THE LIBRARY LADIES of KALAMAZOO

THEIR HOME and HISTORY

Copyright 2016

Library Ladies Group, LLC

Kalamazoo, Michigan

Copyright © 2016 Text by Library Ladies Group, LLC
Copyright © 2016 Photos by Carla J. Noe-Emig

All rights reserved. No part of this publication may be reproduced, distributed, or transmitted in any form or by any means, including photocopying, recording, or other electronic or mechanical methods, without the prior written permission of the publisher, except in the case of brief quotations embodied in critical reviews and certain other noncommercial uses permitted by copyright law. For permission requests, write to the publisher, addressed "Attention: Permissions Coordinator," at the address below.

Library Ladies Group, LLC
813 West South Street • Kalamazoo, Michigan 49007
LibraryLadiesGroup@gmail.com

Ordering Information:
Special discounts are available on quantity purchases by corporations, associations, and for U.S. trade bookstores and wholesalers. For details, contact the publisher.

Cover design by Nick Emig
Book design by Sean Hollins, Fortitude Graphic Design and Printing
Consultant Editor/Publisher Sonya Hollins, Season Press, LLC
Interior photography (excluding historic images) by Carla J. Noe-Emig
Published in collaboration with Season Press, LLC

Library of Congress Control Number: 2016937555

The Library Ladies of Kalamazoo: Their Home and History / Library Ladies Group, LLC

1. Ladies' Library Association —History —Women's History 2. Women's Clubs —Michigan
3. Architecture — History 4. Libraries 5. Kalamazoo

ISBN Paperback: 978-0-9863173-3-0
ISBN Hardbound: 978-0-9863173-1-6

First Edition
10 9 8 7 6 5 4 3 2 1

Printed in the United States of America

Table of Contents

OUR STORY - THE BEGINNINGS	vi
ACKNOWLEDGEMENTS	viii
DEDICATION	x
FOREWORD	xiii
PREFACE	xiv
CHAPTER 1 – LAYING THE GROUNDWORK	2
CHAPTER 2 – INVITING ELEMENTS	12
CHAPTER 3 – ENTRY FOYER	20
CHAPTER 4 – MAIN LIBRARY	28
CHAPTER 5 – LENDING LIBRARY	40
CHAPTER 6 – AUDITORIUM AND SECOND FLOOR	48
CHAPTER 7 – TIMES PAST	60
CHAPTER 8 – 1931 ADDITION	70
CHAPTER 9 – STATUARY	80
CHAPTER 10 – STAINED GLASS	86
CHAPTER 11 – PAINTINGS AND WALL HANGINGS	98
CHAPTER 12 – FURNITURE	116
CHAPTER 13 – BECOMING BARRIER FREE	128
CHAPTER 14 – 21st CENTURY	134
CHAPTER 15 – BASEMENT	146
CHAPTER 16 – GARDEN	150
CHAPTER 17 – SPECIAL CELEBRATIONS	156
CHAPTER 18 – HEART AND SOUL OF LLA	164
TIMELINE CHRONOLOGY (HIGHLIGHTS 1844 TO 2015)	171
GENERAL FEDERATION OF WOMEN'S CLUBS	180
"THE COLLECT" LADIES' LIBRARY ASSOCIATION SONG AND POEM	181
ABOUT THE AUTHORS	185
HISTORICAL ORIGINAL BLUEPRINTS	189
BIBLIOGRAPHY	192
INDEX	198

OUR STORY – THE BEGINNINGS

The Ladies' Library Association building on South Park Street has been a noted feature of downtown Kalamazoo since its construction in 1878-79. It is known as the first building in the nation to be financed and built by and for a women's organization. Almost a century later it was the first structure in the city to be placed on the National Register of Historic Places. The building reflects the influence of European architecture. Today its fine architecture and carefully preserved furnishings offer the community a window into the past. Careful renovations have preserved the historic character of the site, which is now barrier-free.

The original group of women first met as a reading / sewing circle in 1844, only 13 years after the founding of the village of Bronson (later renamed Kalamazoo). These women, mostly from New England and upstate New York, envisioned a community that valued education and culture. By 1852, their numbers had grown and they were formally organized as the Ladies' Library Association (LLA). Noted founding member Lucinda Hinsdale Stone furthered the ideal of creating "a college for women." The LLA sponsored lectures and formed the first circulating library in the region. It was to remain active for over 20 years, until the founding of the public library. The club expanded its services to help Kalamazoo's growing population with dental clinics and classes on health and hygiene.

The LLA has the distinction of being the first women's club established in Michigan and the third oldest in the United States. It continues to flourish as a nonprofit charitable organization with a steady membership of about 180 women. Membership activities center on support of literacy and women's education, as well as preserving and sharing the LLA's historic home, as a public trust.

While the LLA, including its circulating library, was an active force in the Village, it lacked a permanent site. At various times it was housed in a private home, a fire station, and Corporation Hall (the forerunner of City Hall), among other places. After the Civil War, serious consideration was given to securing property and constructing a building to serve as a library and museum, as well as an auditorium for community use. Treasurer and charter member Ruth Webster donated land for the building on South Park Street, at the time valued at $1,375. From careful management of funds obtained from overdue book fines and loans at interest to local businesses, $3,000 was raised. This permitted the group to begin design and construction. Work on the building began in 1878 and was completed in 1879.

The group sought to create a building worthy of their goal of "promoting moral and educational improvement in the town of Kalamazoo." Chicago architect H. L. Gay created an elaborate design in the fashionable Venetian Gothic style appropriate for fine public buildings. Local builder Frederick Bush was hired to erect the building for $8,000. Once the shell was completed, the club raised another $2,000 to pay for a tiled vestibule, stained-glass work, a stage, and scenery. Furnishings were provided through the generosity of LLA members and friends. The total cost of the building and furnishings was $14,000.

Since 1852, the LLA has carried out its commitment to serving the Kalamazoo community, especially its women and children.

THE LIBRARY LADIES OF KALAMAZOO
Their Home and History

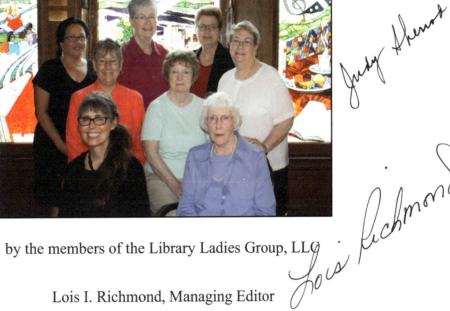

by the members of the Library Ladies Group, LLC

Lois I. Richmond, Managing Editor
Judy Sherrod, Co-Editor
Deborah M. Killarney, Co-Editor
Carla J. Noe-Emig, Photographer
Vanita Aloisio
Barbara Baker
Lisa Salay

Sharon Carlson, Research Consultant

ACKNOWLEDGEMENTS & SPECIAL THANKS TO:

Nick Emig (multi-media artist) for his graphic design work on the book cover, photo editing, restorative works on vintage photos, creation of the Library Ladies of Kalamazoo YouTube channel, and filming / production of CTA video clips.

The late **Dorothy Dykema** for her numerous conversations with the authors, adding to the story of the Ladies' Library Association gleaned from her many years of service with the Association.

Marge Kars and **Richard Baker** for their contributions to content of some chapters.

Lynn Houghton (Curator at Charles C. & Lynn L. Zhang Legacy Collections Center, Western Michigan University Archives and Regional History Collections in Kalamazoo, Michigan) who greatly assisted the process of researching documents in the Archives.

Nelson Nave (Kalamazoo architect, specializing in historical restoration) for his expertise on the LLA building architecture and details.

Sharon Ferraro (Historic Preservation Coordinator for the City of Kalamazoo, Michigan) for her expertise in Kalamazoo history and LLA building architecture and details.

The late **Helen Sheridan** (long-time employee and Director of Collections and Exhibitions at the Kalamazoo Institute of Arts in Kalamazoo, Michigan) and her work "The Art Collection: Stained Glass, Paintings, Sculpture" of 2002, which proved invaluable to our research.

Chris Roussi (Senior Scientist, Michigan Tech Research Institute in Ann Arbor, Michigan) for introducing and guiding the authors through the collaborative authoring software Mercurial.

Sean and **Sonya Hollins** (Fortitude Graphics and Season Press) for their assistance in the final editing and book design.

And to the many members of the Ladies' Library Association who contributed to the spirit of this book through their accomplishments over the years, as well as the numerous meticulous crafts people who worked on the LLA building throughout its history.

DEDICATION

The authors dedicate this book to the past, present and future members of the Ladies' Library Association, so that their mission of enriching others through education, literacy, philanthropy, and volunteerism will continue. We honor those who believed in "Do what you can!" as a simple motto to promote continued community involvement, the preservation of the building and its contents, its traditions, and its National Register of Historic Places designation.

✻ Historic illustration of Ladies' Library building.

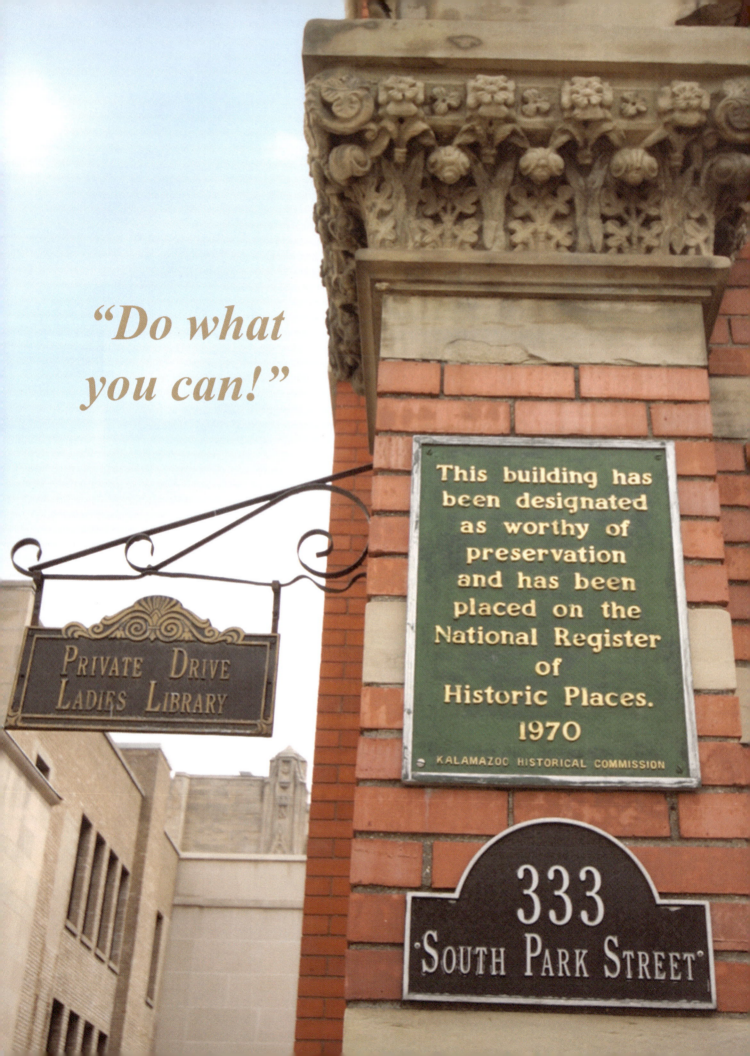

FOREWORD

This pictorial book guides you through the home of the Ladies' Library Association of Kalamazoo (known as the LLA) and its preserved history site. The LLA building was designated as the Michigan Historical Commission Registered Site No. 221 in 1961 and was placed on the National Register of Historic Places in 1970. As you browse through this book, the LLA invites you to sense the warmth of the beautiful wood and the architectural details. Note how light filters through the numerous stained-glass windows throughout the building. Original chandeliers and other historic lamps are prominent. Imagine sipping a cup of tea as you tour.

Think of those who came before you, who labored to share books, helped soldiers during the Civil War, championed health resources for the community, and provided for the general welfare of area citizens. Imagine arriving in a horse-drawn buggy to enjoy a lecture or concert amongst the hustle and bustle of the city's activities. Picture a high tea with women adorned in hats and fancy dresses of lace, velvet, taffeta, and other fine fabrics who are conversing with each other about daily events. Visualize a table set with silver service, crystal stemware, and linens with a theme-related centerpiece or seasonal flowers.

The building provides an environment that is meant to invite members and guests to a quieter time, to enjoy each other's company, and to reflect on the simple beauty of its historic significance. The joy is realized when different generations from a membership of 180 get together.

Any woman who is interested in this organization is welcome to become a member. Members support diversity. The simple motto of yesterday "Do what you can" holds true today. The authors, members of the LLA, welcome you now to enjoy the visual pleasures of its home and learn of the history and accomplishments of those women and their organization.

❋ Page xii: National historic site marker.   ❋ Page xiii: Michigan historic site marker.

xiii

PREFACE

Kalamazoo in the 1840s

By the time that Mrs. Alexis Ransom and Mrs. Lyman Kendall decided to spend one afternoon a week reading to each other in 1844, the village of Kalamazoo had grown considerably from its founding in 1829 by Titus Bronson. Between 1830 and 1840, the population of Michigan had multiplied almost seven times (Dunbar 1952, 40). In 1846, the *Kalamazoo Gazette* published this assessment of Kalamazoo –

> "The streets are constantly filled with teams, and the sidewalks are crowded with persons passing and repassing all intent on some object of pursuit. Boxes, bales and crates of merchandise are beheld in every direction; and the ceaseless sound of many hammers gives evidence of the rapid growth of our village" (Schmitt 1976, 7).

Movement into Michigan was greatly facilitated by the opening of the Erie Canal in 1823. Many of the early settlers arrived from New England and they came with Yankee attitude and determination. "They were determined to establish here a flourishing agricultural center and a city, with schools, churches, stores and mills" (Dunbar 1952, 27). A sawmill was established very early, making it possible for most of the houses being erected of sawn lumber rather than logs. In 1848, James Fenimore Cooper wrote in his book, *Oak Openings*, the following:

> "We left the railroad at Kalamazoo – an unusually pretty village, on the banks of the stream of that name. Those who laid out this place, some fifteen years since, had the taste to preserve most of its trees; and the houses and grounds that stand a little apart from the busiest streets – and they are numerous for a place of rather more than two thousand souls – are particularly pleasant to the eye, on account of the shade, and the rural pictures they present" (Schmitt 1976, 33).

Mid-century Kalamazoo was a lively and interesting place to live. It was a time when a great deal of wealth could be accumulated for those with the ingenuity to take advantage of the opportunities available, not only in the village of Kalamazoo but also in the state of Michigan. This wealth afforded many residents leisure time to be able to pursue a variety of activities. There were educational opportunities, many churches, lodges, clubs, lectures, traveling shows, horse racing and celebrations (Dunbar 1952, 87).

Interest in politics was high. In the time span of 1840-59, Kalamazoo produced a chief justice of the state supreme court, a governor, a United States senator, and three members of Congress (Dunbar 1952, 64). The early settlers of Kalamazoo laid the foundation for a city that would be known for its support of education, cultural activities, and political action.

❋ Early archived LLA record books.

Lucinda Stone

Woman… Mother of Clubs… Teacher… Leader… Writer… Mother… Wife…. These are just a few words that begin to define Lucinda Hinsdale Stone, one of the founding members of the LLA. She was the youngest of 12 children born to Aaron Hinsdale and Lucinda Mitchell (Hinsdale) in Hinesburg, Vermont. Education and teaching became the main focuses of her life's work and helped shape the person she was to become as a woman living in the 19th century. Her strong influence on the Ladies' Library Association of Kalamazoo carries through to the present, albeit, in the grand scheme of her life, it is but a small part of her legacy.

Dr. James Stone and Lucinda Hinsdale were married in 1840 after he finished his studies at the Andover Theological Seminary. They moved to Kalamazoo in 1843. He was sent to a small Baptist Church and was also put in charge of the University of Michigan branch located in Kalamazoo. Lucinda Stone began teaching there part-time and eventually became the head of the Ladies' Department at what was to become Kalamazoo College.

She was considered one of the best teachers of her time and stated, "I think few teachers have loved their work as I have … and I wish to insist here that the life of a true teacher may be full of noble enjoyment" (Perry 1902, 48-49). Teaching was her lifelong work and she particularly cared about providing education to women. She was instrumental in getting a bill introduced in 1869, allowing women to attend the University of Michigan (Potts and Lyons-Jenness 1997, 20).

A turn of events occurred at the college for Lucinda after nearly 20 years of teaching. Her methods and ideas were considered radical for the times. Her progressive thinking and her support of coeducation and women's suffrage, both controversial subjects, made the trustees at the college increasingly critical of her and of her husband. The resistance to Lucinda and Dr. Stone met its inevitable end on November 5, 1863, when they submitted their resignations.

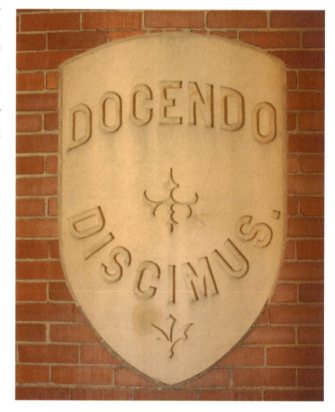

✳ Latin phrase "By teaching we learn," carved in stone and mounted into the brick of the LLA building.

✳ Images of Lucinda Stone throughout her life.

✶ Lucinda Hinsdale Stone is buried in the Mountain Home Cemetery in Kalamazoo, Michigan.

Her resignation came during the middle of the Civil War and was the beginning of a new phase of life for Lucinda. As one of the founders of the Ladies' Library Association in 1852 and having been elected to the Board of Directors, her involvement in the organization only enhanced her vision for the club and pushed her to work harder. The library remained open during the war with an evening reading class started with Lucinda being one of the readers.

The years after the war were busy for Lucinda. She became involved with the formation of many different women's clubs, earning her the nickname "Mother of Clubs." She was solicited to organize classes in other cities, most of which grew into permanent clubs too numerous to mention here. She wrote a column called "Club Talks" for the *Detroit Post and Tribune* with an audience of thousands (Perry 1902, 163). Her love of travel and art and the contributions she made to the library are outlined in later chapters.

The legacy of Lucinda Hinsdale Stone is her passion, her tenacity, and her tireless work, not only for women of the Ladies' Library Association, but also for the city of Kalamazoo. Susan B. Anthony said, "…women of the nation and the world owe her very much for her persistent efforts to secure the perfect equalities of educational opportunities for girls" (Perry 1902, 160).

Since 1852, the women of the Ladies' Library Association of Kalamazoo have carefully told her story and kept the memory of her formidable contributions alive. The LLA is fortunate to see how all these characteristics culminated into a force of strength and progress for women and for the organization. Who do we have today as such a role model? Perhaps it is best summed up from a quote by a former president of the Kalamazoo Twentieth Century Club, "…We ne'er shall see her like again" (Perry 1902, 171).

The Civil War

Although the first men in Kalamazoo County were not drafted until the winter of 1865, the role of the Ladies' Library Association during the Civil War began at the outset in 1861 (Durant 1880). The United States Sanitary Commission was created by the Federal Government to provide medical assistance to soldiers during the Civil War. The Soldiers Aid Societies supported the Commission by raising funds and collecting supplies to send to military hospitals. The LLA members formed the Ladies' Soldiers Aid Society and went to work making blankets and clothing as well as preserved food, all of which were to go to Union soldiers.

During the late summer of 1864, Mrs. John (Ruth) Potter and Miss Eliza Fisher proposed the idea of holding a "Michigan State Sanitary Fair" for the sole purpose of raising money to aid the sick, wounded, and disabled soldiers. The success was not only due through the efforts of local citizens, but also those of people throughout the state of Michigan. The four-day event raised $9,300 over expenses and was recognized by the Adjutant General of the State of Michigan (Durant 1880, 235). This amount of money is equivalent to $136,194.21 today (Inflation Calculator n.d.).

Chapter 1: *Laying the Groundwork*

"She hath wrought a good work."
-- from the Ruth Webster Memorial Window

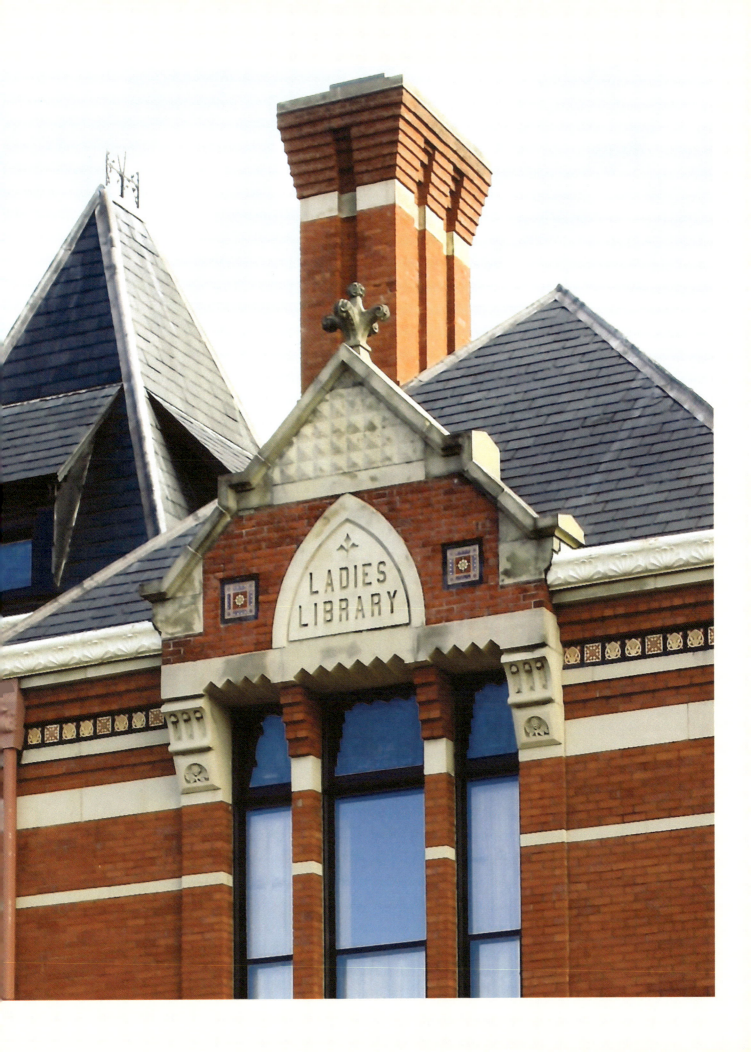

Ruth Webster

As one of the founding mothers of the Ladies' Library Association, Mrs. D. B. Webster played several key roles. She was appointed to the first Board of Directors. Later she was elected treasurer, holding that position for over 24 years. Starting in 1864 she also served as the Association librarian for 15 years (Potts and Lyons-Jenness 1997, 10). She was energetic in those duties—keeping meticulous book circulation records, personally dusting books and shelves, and even learning how to repair the bindings of books. Also notable is the fact that she managed the building fund, influenced others to increase its growth, and donated the building site at 333 South Park Street (originally purchased by her family and valued at $1,375). She was adamant in her support of a permanent home for the LLA.

Mrs. Webster was born in Scipio, New York. Her father was a businessman and Ruth performed clerical duties for him. She first married Daniel Thomas. Her only child was born to them, but died at age 14 of heart disease. After her first husband passed, she married Judge D. B. Webster, whom she also outlived (*Kalamazoo Gazette* 1878).

On November 27, 1878, Lucinda Stone wrote: "Mrs. Webster was told by the builder of the new edifice if she would watch from her window that afternoon she would see the first smoke rise from the furnace they were putting in, and which would indicate to her the approaching completion of the building." Mrs. Webster did indeed watch with joy. Seeing the wisps of smoke rising from the chimney must have given her a great feeling of accomplishment and contentment. That very night, she died peacefully at her dressing table at age 69

✳ Ruth Webster's entombment located to the left of the Webster family marker.

(Pioneer Society of the State of Michigan 1881, 532-535). She is buried in Kalamazoo's Mountain Home Cemetery within sight of Lucinda Hinsdale Stone's grave.

Style, Architecture, Land Ownership, Price

The first notion that the ladies of the LLA wished to own a dedicated building came in 1855. At that time Ruth Webster offered a lot next to her home on South Rose Street, if they decided to build (Potts and Lyons-Jenness 1997, 13). The offer was not accepted. Over the next few years, Mrs. Webster offered land twice more. Other downtown lots were also considered for the building site. Finally in 1872, the Board approved an offer by Mrs. Webster of a Park Street lot, the current site of the LLA building.

As treasurer, Mrs. Webster was also in charge of the building fund. Monies increased through library dues; ice cream and strawberry socials; domestic, literary, and scientific lectures; concerts; raffles; and interest on loans (mostly to members' husbands at a rate of 10%). By 1877 the fund grew to $3,814 (Potts and Lyons-Jenness 1997, 29-30).

Prior to 1879, a woman could not legally own land unless she inherited it through dower rights when her husband died (Leiby 2010). Even then she might have to share the land inheritance with her children, especially with her sons. As Mrs. Webster was a widow with no children, she wholly owned land through dower rights. She could not, however, legally give the property to the women of the LLA. No husband or dower rights were involved in this situation.

A change in Michigan law regarding women solely owning property had to be enacted. Kalamazoo's Lansing representative the Honorable J. Parsons had a key role in obtaining passage of the bill (LLA 1880 Annual Meeting Minutes 1881). With his support and the encouragement of LLA members' husbands who were judges, legislators, and other influential personages, the ladies were confident this formal step would come to fruition. Plans for construction began in earnest in 1878.

The original building was to be of modest wood construction. However, after four fires of wood structures caused much destruction in the village, it was deemed that no future public building would be designed of wood. Henry L. Gay, a Chicago architect and friend to several LLA members, was hired to produce architectural drawings of a brick building. His fee was $75. Later, Mr. Gay designed the downstairs wall cabinets and the upstairs stage for an additional $25 (Potts and Lyons-Jenness 1997, 30-31).

The original edifice was primarily 30' x 60', and a composite of architectural styles. Most

often it is referred to as Venetian Gothic (Houghton and O'Connor 2001, 174) (Carlson 2002) with its lancet arches and Byzantine and Moorish influences. There are also flourishes of Queen Anne (Schmitt 1976) (Carlson 2002) in its irregular pitched roof, corner tower, and shadowed entry. Gay's plans were accepted on August 17, 1878.

Local contractors Bush and Paterson were chosen to erect the building, exclusive of stained-glass windows, lighting, and interior decorating. The final building costs were $14,000. This included $8,000 in construction expenses and $6,000 for furnishings. Additional amounts were raised to pay for tile in the vestibule, windows, gas fixtures, bookcases and cabinets, exterior work, and the stage (LLA Board of Directors Meeting Minutes 1878). The ladies were much a part of the planning process. They were also thrifty, arranging for used carpet from a local church to be taken up and re-laid on the first floor.

With the unexpected death of Mrs. Webster, a stained-glass window was designed in her memory. It honors her role as long-time custodian and champion of the building fund and her donation of the land upon which the LLA building stands. This elaborate window was installed shortly after construction and is described in more detail in Chapter 10.

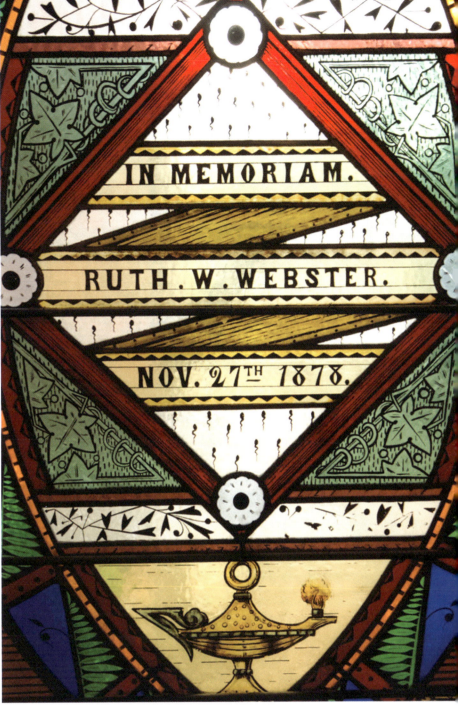

✳ Page 6 top right: 1878 foundation stone; below: Early photo of LLA building.

✳ Page 7 right: Ruth Webster memorial window; left: Ruth Webster's service history.

An Act

To authorize the Ladies Library Association of Kalamazoo to hold property, real and personal, to any amount not exceeding thirty thousand dollars in addition to the value of its books.

Section 1. The People of the State of Michigan enact That the Ladies Library Association of Kalamazoo shall have power and is hereby authorized to hold property, real and personal, to any amount not exceeding thirty thousand dollars in addition to the value of its books.

Section 2. This act shall take immediate effect.

Alonzo Sessions
President of the Senate.
John T. Rich
Speaker of the House of Representatives

Approved May 3, 1879
Charles M. Croswell

❋ The official Act of the Legislature of May 3, 1879.

STATE OF MICHIGAN, } ss.
Office of the Secretary of State.

I, Wm Jenney, Secretary of State of the State of Michigan, DO HEREBY CERTIFY, that I have compared the annexed copy of *An Act of the Legislature of 1879*

with the original *as Enrolled and now on file in this office* and that it is a true and correct transcript therefrom, and of the whole of such original.

In Testimony Whereof, I have hereunto set my hand and affixed the Great Seal of the State of Michigan, at Lansing, this 5th day of May in the year of our Lord one thousand eight hundred and seventy nine.

Secretary of State.

❋ May 5, 1879 filing documentation of the Act.

Construction of the building was completed in November 1878. The official Act of the Legislature of May 3, 1879 states,

> "The people of the State of Michigan enact. [*sic*] That the Ladies' Library Association of Kalamazoo shall have power and is hereby authorized to hold property, real and personal, to any amount not exceeding thirty thousand dollars in addition to the value of its books."

This was a significant milestone in women's history in Michigan and in the United States of America. Formal dedication of the building was held on May 20, 1879. The entire original debt was paid by January 1883 (LLA 1882 Annual Report 1883).

Alley Agreement

An alley separated the LLA building and a residence to the north, giving access from the street to the east property line. It is a charming picture to think of a horse and buggy using this pathway to get to the parking area at the rear of the building.

In December of 1904, the Ladies' Library Association and Laura V. Wagner, the individual who represented the residence, reached an agreement on the common use of the alley. The two parties agreed to share this eight-foot wide passageway. The common driveway would be used as a thoroughfare for foot passengers, teams, and vehicles. This agreement still exists today. Now it is between the Kalamazoo Civic Theatre (which replaced the residence) and the LLA. They continue to share expenses and maintenance of this alley.

❋ Alley easement sign.

Chapter 2: *Inviting Elements*

"A truly great book should be read in youth, again in maturity, and once more in old age, as a fine building should be seen by morning light, at noon, and midnight."

-- Robertson Davies (Canadian author)

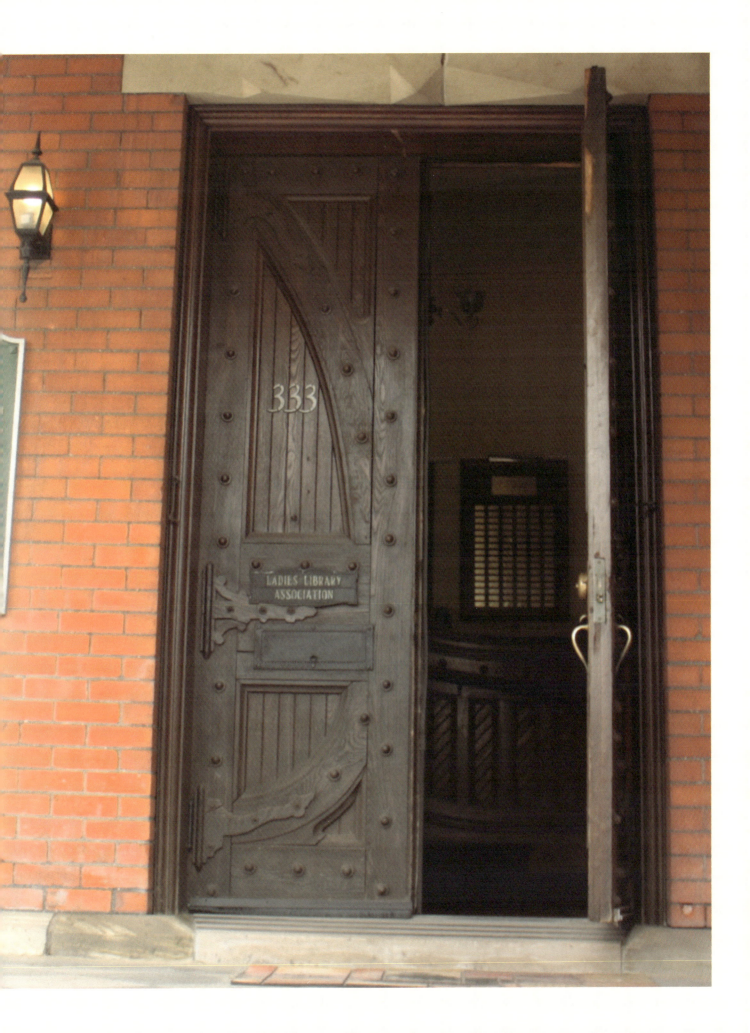

Walking up to the building, one is first struck by its beauty and its details, each having a story to tell. Limestone, copper, cement, iron, to name a few, all come together hopefully evoking enough curiosity in the visitor to want to learn more about this downtown treasure.

❋ Left: Mail slot; above: Brass address numerals.

Angle Brackets

There are two angle brackets on the front entrance columns. The bottom portion, which resembles a cross, has been described as Gothic Revival in style (Andover's Architectural Styles n.d.). Little information is available about these brackets. Kalamazoo architect, Nelson Nave, said they were designed for two reasons. One was to hold up the round rod on the columns and the other was for decorative purposes, to move the eyes away from the rod.

❋ Bottom: Circular rod support; middle: Bracket detail; top: Decorative angle bracket.

✳ Front porch cement tiles; below: Three examples of decorative limestone detail.

Cement Tiles

The cement tiles on the front porch were made by Kalamazoo Cement Works, which was established in 1872. This style of tile dates back to 1824, when a bricklayer in Leeds, England, named Joseph Aspdin patented a cement made by combining clay with limestone through burning and grinding. He called it Portland cement because it resembled stone obtained from the Portland quarries in England. Similar cement tiles laid out in the same pattern can be found at the Receiving Vault at the Mountain Home Cemetery.

Limestone

Early blueprints of the building show that the architect placed brick and limestone in the plans. Limestone is a very common sedimentary rock consisting of calcium carbonate (more than 50%) (Sand Atlas n.d.). It is similar to brick in that it is a masonry product and can be used in load bearing applications. The majority of the good limestone comes from the Bedford, Indiana area.
It is almost always the architect's decision whether or not to use limestone. The rationale is to use it in traditional old details or as a detail that stands out from the brick. It is often used in borders, accents, bases, sills, window heads, columns, and steps.

Today, cast stone is used more often than limestone because it is less expensive. This stone is man-made and contains limestone dust and cement, or other stone dust. It is pushed and hammered into a mold. Some of the stone on the LLA is neither limestone nor brick, but some other kind of aggregate. This can be observed on either side of the front steps. It remains a mystery whether or not it is cast stone (Nave 2015).

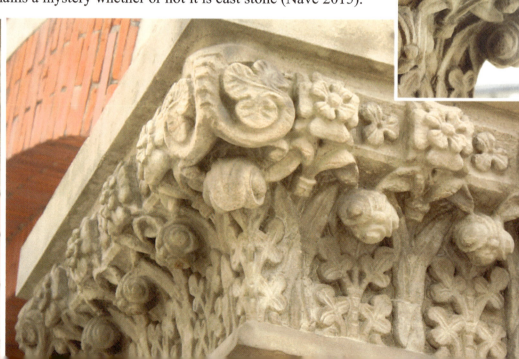

Metal Handrails

The origins of the metal handrails on the front steps can be traced back to the initial construction. Early photographs show that they first appear as a cast iron fence on the top of the roof edge. They were either brought down or fell off and later made into handrails. They were originally straight and horizontal and, at some point, were cut and pieced together to form the railings. Looking at them today, one can see where they were cut and welded together, and later sunk or connected into the steps. Finally, the top handrail was added and painted (Nave 2015). It was most recently painted in 2008 (LLA 2007-2008 House Committee Annual Report 2008).

The exact time frame of this transformation is not known. It is known from the original blueprints that iron hand-railings were not part of the plan. However, it is not until 1949 that the first photos show the building with handrails (*Kalamazoo Gazette* 1949).

Turn Knob To Ring Bell

Mechanical Doorbell

Mechanical doorbells during the time of the construction were made of cast bronze with a cast iron frame, cast iron lever, and back plate. They are also called "twist" doorbells because of the motion the wrist is required to make in order to ring the bell. This style of doorbell mounts through the door. The turn is on the outside and the bell is on the interior (House of Antique Hardware n.d.). One cannot judge the age of a building by its doorbell because the electric version was used as early as 1931. When taking a tour, ask the docent to ring the bell and be charmed by one more element of the LLA building.

Replica Gargoyle

The original gargoyle (described in Chapter 4) was replaced in 1978, during the 1974-1980 restoration. Mr. Lee Wallace of Portage, Michigan, designed and constructed the replica gargoyle. The cost of this was $200. This replica gargoyle was constructed out of copper and was hung on the front porch in June of 1978. It was dedicated in memory of Blanche Billingham, who was an active member in many Kalamazoo organizations, including the Ladies' Library Association. She worked as the secretary / treasurer for her husband's architectural firm. A compilation of her favorite recipes was sold as a fundraiser to aid the restoration project (LLA Historical Restoration Program 1974-1980).

Chapter 3

Entry Foyer

"The atmosphere breathes rest and comfort and the many chambers seem full of welcome."

– Henry Wadsworth Longfellow (from the book *Masque of Pandora*)

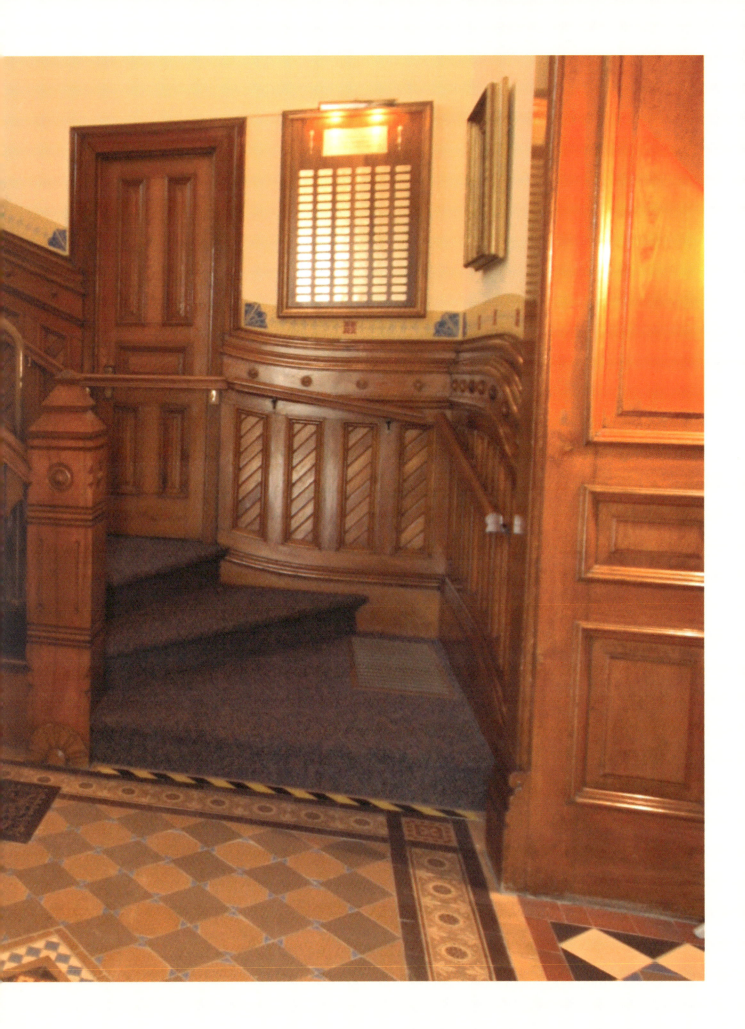

✱ Top: Vestibule staircase; bottom left: Entry door hardware; bottom right: Foyer wainscoting.

✻ Top: Dark ash wainscoting detail; middle right: Newel post; middle left: Newel post carved cap detail; lower middle and bottom: Patterned entryway floor tile.

In a timeless visual language, the building's massive and impressive front doors beckon strangers to enter the vestibule foyer, which extends the first warm welcome to the building. Its design, with beautiful architectural appointments, communicates genial salutations to all who enter.

The Eastlake styling of the skillfully carved fine, dark ash woodwork, wainscoting, and banisters was an elegant simplification of the prevailing Victorian sophistication. The shallow-relief, geometric motif is both aesthetically pleasing and allows for easy cleaning. The same is true of the colorfully patterned tile entryway floor. Originally linoleum had been suggested for this floor because of its popularity and cost-savings. Ultimately this was rejected in favor of ceramic tile, which, even after a century and a half, remains vivid and attractive (LLA Board of Directors Meeting Minutes 1878).

The building was not intended to serve a single age, but rather to span generations, housing them in their shared pursuits of knowledge, enrichment, and enlightenment. As one ascends the 20 stairs and three landings to reach the second floor, the eye is drawn from one form of artistry to the next. A lively hand-painted snowflake pattern runs the entire length to the second story, bordering the wainscoting. Panels of meticulously cut and matched stained-glass windows face the north. Near the top of the stairwell, on the west wall, is a lovely triangular stained-glass window bearing the letters "L L A" that is original to 1878. Photos of this signet window are often used as the logo for the Association on small flyers or brochures.

❋ Page 24: Archive photo of entry foyer with original stained-glass window and gas light fixture.

❋ Page 25 left: Staircase landing leading to second floor; top right: Hand-stenciled border above stairwell wainscoting; bottom right: LLA signet stained-glass window located in stairwell tower.

❋ Page 26 top: Domed tower ceiling; bottom left: Ceiling view from foyer; bottom right: Domed tower stained-glass detail.

Without argument, the crown jewel is the domed tower ceiling with an authentic star-scattered fresco (paint on wet plaster) treatment. This same treatment was used above the stage in the Richmond Auditorium. With very pleasing results, the domes were cleaned and preserved with a special formulation during the restoration effort that began in 1974, supervised by Louis and Annette Conti, local preservationists (LLA Historical Restoration Program 1974-1980). At times, sunlight from the peak windows creates a kaleidoscope of brilliant colors that dance through and across the deep recesses, prompting feelings of awe in the viewer.

To enter the building is to be invited to experience all that the Ladies' Library Association has to offer generations of the past, present, and future.

❋ Page 27 top: Foyer light fixture; bottom right: Past Presidents' plaque; middle: Vintage umbrella stand; bottom left: "old-fashioned brass doorbell" donated by LLA member Bernadine Endsley, December 1977.

Chapter 4

Main Library

"Around here, however, we don't look backwards for very long. We keep moving forward, opening new doors and doing new things, because we are curious...."

-- Walt Disney (American entrepreneur and cartoonist)

✳ Page 30/31 top: Archive photo of main library room; bottom: Librarian's brass bell.

On March 12, 1852, the Ladies' Library Association opened the first lending or subscription library in the village of Kalamazoo. It remained the only public library in the village until the Kalamazoo Public Library opened in 1872.

An LLA goal was formally declared in the *1858 Constitution of the Ladies' Library Association*. It states:

> "The object of this Association shall be the establishment and maintenance of a Library; to afford and encourage useful and entertaining reading; to furnish literary and scientific lectures; and other means of promoting moral and educational improvement in the town of Kalamazoo" (Potts and Lyons-Jenness 1997, Book Jacket).

Initially the library was housed in the home of Colonel George Rice, brother of member Susan Rice. The Rice home was soon overwhelmed and the book collection moved to a small room above the Austin & Tomlinson store. Next, space was rented in the courthouse and in 1856 it moved to the basement of the First Baptist Church. In 1867, village trustees offered two large rooms in the Fireman's Hall on Burdick Street (today occupied by V&A Bootery). The LLA lending library remained there for the next five years (Potts and Lyons-Jenness 1997, 9, 17, 29-30).

During LLA building construction, the book collection and cabinets were again stored in the First Baptist Church. Finally, upon completion of the building in 1879, the collection was permanently moved to the ground floor in the main library room. A circulation desk, where the librarian checked books in and out, was located in the southwest corner of that room. The original brass desk bell used by the librarian remains on display at the library.

The annual subscription fee was initially fifty cents and later increased to one dollar. Each sub-

scriber (man or woman) had his or her name recorded in the librarian's book of registry. Anyone who was not a member could pay a fee of twenty-five cents per month for "the privilege of borrowing books" (LLA 1891 Constitution 1891). Members and non-members could borrow books for two weeks. A borrower was fined one dime for each week that a book was overdue and paid for any loss or injury to a book.

Books were added to the collection by purchase and donation. By 1879, the collection grew to over 2,000 books. Each new book had to pass review by the LLA Board. This meant "all works shall be, if not of a high moral tone, at least as such as shall work no injury to morals

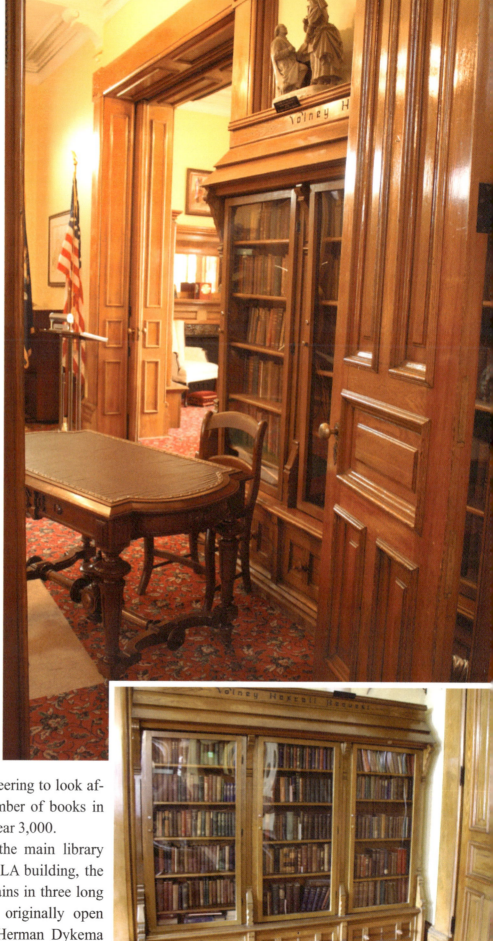

✳ Entry door from foyer to main library room; below: Bookcase holding volumes from original collection.

or good sense" (LLA Board Minutes January 1859). The collection included books on science, art, poetry, history, theology, encyclopedias, novels, and "standard works and modern effusions" (LLA 1858 Annual Report January 1859). Minutes of monthly board meetings reflect lists of books accepted by the Board.

Although the LLA continued to add books, magazines and government documents to the collection, use of the lending library declined with the creation of the Kalamazoo Public Library. For many years, up to 600 books were circulated annually. By 1909 the number of books circulated dwindled to 62. In 1908 the Board felt the Association no longer needed the services of a paid librarian; members would take turns volunteering to look after the library. The total number of books in the library at that time was near 3,000.

Today when you enter the main library on the ground floor of the LLA building, the vintage book collection remains in three long wood bookcases. Although originally open shelved, by the year 2000 Herman Dykema

※ Top left: Leather-bound works by Dickens; top right: Period hand-carved easel; bottom: Library steps for retrieving books from high shelves.

(husband of longtime member Dorothy Dykema and in 2008 became an honorary male LLA member) had placed wood backings and lockable glass doors on each case (LLA 1999 House & Grounds Annual Report 2000).

Many treasures remain in these bookcases–some familiar, some not. A close look reveals Dickens, along with Robert and Elizabeth Barrett Browning, Longfellow, George Eliot, and Emerson. Also displayed are *Morning Glories* by Louisa May Alcott, 1873; *Decorum: A Practical Treatise on Etiquette and Dress*, 1878; *The Woman in White* by Wilkie Collins, 1871; *Last of the Mohicans* by James Fenimore Cooper, 1859; and *Troy and its Remains* by Henry Schlieman, 1875. These volumes stand in tribute and testament to the women of the LLA who gave the village of Kalamazoo its first public library.

❋ Ruth Webster memorial window panels.

34

✳ Top left: Chandelier with ceiling medallion; top right: Brass chandelier detail; bottom right: Warm glow of lit chandelier; bottom left: Etched glass on chandelier globe.

❋ Original gargoyle now located in the main library room.

The Original Gargoyle on the Ladies' Library Building

The Ladies' Library building is believed to have the only attached gargoyle in the city of Kalamazoo. The gift from Miss Anna D. Clark, dean of girls at Kalamazoo Central High School in 1904, is believed to have been purchased in England and comes from a 12th century cathedral. The purpose of the gargoyle is to direct water, like a drainpipe, from the higher roofs away from the building walls so the lower walls are not damaged.

Gargoyles come in many shapes of birds, animals, and humans, often grotesque in features. The word comes from the French word *gargo* meaning throat. Gargoyles are much more popular in Europe than in the United States. In the U.S., gargoyles can be found on churches and other significant buildings in big cities. They serve a very useful purpose and provide some mystery with their presence.

The gargoyle on the LLA building was stolen in 1961 and returned in 1962—a mystery still unsolved. The grotesque bird-like figure was returned in three pieces. It was left in a crate on the porch with a note indicating the person that returned the gargoyle was not the person who stole it. A replica was made and installed on the porch by Lee Wallace, a gentleman from Portage, Michigan. The original, after being returned, was repaired by Corwin Rife, curator of exhibits at the Kalamazoo Public Museum and placed inside the building for safekeeping. This gargoyle now stands sentry over the LLA's books, statuary, and other items of value and beauty.

The *Kalamazoo Gazette*, a local newspaper, wrote three articles about the incident of the stolen gargoyle. In 2014 Lois Richmond, a member of the LLA, wrote and published a book of historical fiction, *The Missing Gargoyle of the Ladies' Library*. Today, both of the LLA gargoyles are honored as significant features of the building and fulfill their duties daily. As a drainpipe outside, one gargoyle is a symbol of protection. The original is a symbol of good will inside the building.

❋ Page 37: Replica gargoyle currently installed on the roof of the front porch.

Yellow Roses

The symbol of the Ladies' Library Association is the yellow rose. It is significant that this symbol was chosen since yellow roses represent feelings of friendship and optimism. This hearkens to the beginning of the Association when the eight women who founded the LLA cemented their friendship by establishing the first lending library in the village. With limited opportunities for women to assert themselves publicly, their optimism to take on this project was admirable. Throughout the history of the LLA, that optimism would be tested again and again as finances, controversy, leaky roofs, and strong personalities would become a part of the fabric of the Association.

The yellow rose is also the symbol of the General Federation of Women's Club (GFWC). Given that the LLA took on much of the structure and causes of the GFWC, it is likely that the symbol was also adopted by the LLA in solidarity with that national organization.

The yellow rose has significance to the Women's Suffrage Movement as well. "In an age before telephones, radio, and television, the use of color served as an instant means of visual recognition and became vividly symbolic in the suffrage movement" (National Women's History Museum, n.d.). The use of the color gold began with Susan B. Anthony and Elizabeth Cady Stanton's 1867 campaign to pass a state suffrage referendum in Kansas. They chose as a symbol, the Kansas sunflower. Thereafter, the color gold became associated with the suffrage movement. "Suffrage supporters used gold pins, ribbons, sashes, and yellow roses to denote their cause" (National Women's History Museum n.d.). With this history and the strong suffragette opinions of women such as Lucinda Hinsdale Stone, it is not surprising that the Ladies' Library Association would adopt the yellow rose as its symbol.

❋ Page 38: Yellow roses, symbol of the LLA.

❋ Page 39: clockwise from top left: Wall sconce on east wall of main library room; library bookcase drawer pull; decorative door knob; wooden window shutters; cast Victorian shutter lock; and carved baseboard trim.

Chapter 5
Lending Library

"I'm curious and I love being curious. I like knowing things about the world that we're living in."
-- Robert Redford
(from the film *Walk in the Woods*)

✳ *Lines of Knowledge* window panels and close-up details.

From the main room, continue west through tall wood pocket doors into a cozy alcove. Over the years, this space was used for numerous functions including Board of Directors and committee meetings, a parlor, and a museum. The beautiful stained-glass window here, titled *Lines of Knowledge*, faces Park Street at the front of the building. Read more about this window in Chapter 10.

During its time as a museum, various annual Board and museum committee minutes listed collected artifacts housed in this space. These items were donated and consigned to the LLA, as it was considered a suitable place for exhibition and safekeeping. Displayed were archeological, geological, and natural history specimens; articles of historic value; and *objets d'art* of various kinds.

Curiosities included a honeycomb coral; Missouri onyx; a Mexican water cooler; a pair of Indian leggings; a collection of articles used in Hin Doo [*sic*] worship; a Venus flower basket; a buffalo tooth; stuffed birds, nests and eggs; butterflies, moths, and other insects in well-classified condition; lava from Mauna Loa in Hawaii; and a chunk of Plymouth Rock. Some of the paper relics included an envelope constructed from returned greenbacks, old colonial stamped paper, General Jackson's autograph, and a statistical atlas.

The Board minutes of January 8, 1881, state, "an effort was made to secure for the library a contribution from the Smithsonian Institute, which was so far successful as to gain for the library a complete set of its 'Miscellaneous Collections' excepting three volumes now out of print, and a promise of contributions to the museum hereafter." The 'Miscellaneous Collections' were a series of quarterly periodicals published to note administrative and scholarly achievements of the Smithsonian Institute. The LLA museum appears to have earned a distinguished reputation.

During the 2013 renovation, a box of seashells was found in the basement of the LLA building. At one time they were undoubtedly displayed in the museum. On a small piece of paper in the box the

words "Peck Collection" were written. Research with the Kalamazoo Valley Museum determined the shells were part of the larger Peck Shell Collection housed there. The shells were returned to the public museum to complete the original collection.

Although a formal museum does not currently exist, in 2014 the LLA started a collection of vintage women's clothing and unique acces-

✻ Archive photos of lending library alcove.

※ Wardrobe with vintage clothing and accessories collection, featuring black velvet dress worn by Lillian Grierson (aunt of donors James and Lois Richmond); top right: Green beaded dress worn by Irene Chadborn (grandmother of donor Barbara Baker); bottom right: Cord and hand-embroidered detail on a collection dress.

sories. Many items were donated by member Jerre James from her personal collection. A cedar-lined wardrobe cabinet also was donated to hold and protect the articles. Grace Anne Kalafut assumed responsibility of this project. She critiques new additions to the collection and sets up displays at teas, luncheons, and other events. These items offer a glimpse into the past and stimulate interesting conversation among members and visitors.

Today, this alcove room is called the lending library and it is used primarily as a circulating library for LLA members. It is furnished with two large bookcases—one original and another matching case installed in 2003 by Herm Dykema (LLA 2002-2003 House Committee Annual Report 2003). Now

* Lending library fireplace and time capsule plaque.

more contemporary reading materials are offered here. Although not limited to any specific topics, many books have women-related issues or authors, are about Kalamazoo history, or are written by local authors.

A focal point in this alcove is the impressive fireplace. The hearth was installed in 1888 for $77.12 (Potts and Lyons-Jenness 1997, 38). Its design includes an ornately carved and mirrored mantel. The firebox is surrounded with green-hued majolica glazed tile, popular in the late 1800s. The tile design includes a young woman listening to a minstrel, a gargoyle-type bird, and patterns of nature.

Now the fireplace is decorative only and hides a secret. As part of the 150th anniversary celebration of the founding of the LLA, a time capsule was placed in the firebox. Among other items, the capsule contains the "2002 LLA annual report, a photo of the 2002 Board of Directors and other documents." The time capsule will be opened in May 2052 (LLA 2001-2002 President's Report 2002).

In the building's architectural drawings of July 31, 1878, plans designated a circle with "W B" (wash basin) on the left side of the fireplace. Although there are no known photos, this is a record of a water source (or at least water drainage) in the original construction. It may have been used for light food preparation or cleanup during ice cream socials and teas, when refreshments were brought into the building to share following public events.

The LLA June 1879 minutes reveal there was "much discussion on moving the basin to the basement or covering it with suitable appointments to the room." Several other meeting minutes reveal that

water pipes were often frozen and leaked. It is not known exactly, but this water source was likely removed during the kitchen addition in 1931.

Initially there was no separate "closet" space in the drawings on the north side of this alcove. At the January 15, 1900 LLA meeting, the president's report contains brief remarks regarding the installation of a new lavatory and cloakroom for a cost of $287 (Potts and Lyons-Jenness 1997, 49). Since many community groups used the building on a weekly basis, a safe was purchased between 1935 and 1936 to protect LLA's important papers and silver service. It was placed in this closet space where it was locked and out of public view.

The original door to the closet was hinged and often in the way of members and guests wanting to enter the room. In 1999, a tall pocket-door replaced the hinged door, again installed by Herm Dykema. The safe was moved to the basement of the building and the silver was stored in a new locked cabinet created in the kitchen under the stairway.

Currently this small closet is used for storage of tables, folding chairs, audiovisual equipment, and printed information about the Ladies' Library. Open coat racks and hat shelves were added just outside this closet area.

✻ Door to 1900 cloak room addition.

Chapter 6
Auditorium and Second Floor

"The conductor stepped up, tapped twice on the rostrum, and a great hush descended. I felt the stillness, the auditorium alive, expectant."
-- Jojo Moyes
(from the film *Me Before You*)

✷ Archive photos of auditorium.

T he 1931 addition to the LLA building greatly enhanced its function. On the lower level, a large kitchen was added as well as a small powder room. On the second floor, another powder room, two dressing rooms, and a storage room (now the President's Room) completed the addition. The dressing rooms were intended for the use of the lecturers or entertainers performing in the auditorium. In later years they became a place for bridal parties to dress, as the building became a popular venue to hold weddings. Over the years, a minimal amount of updating went into the rooms.

When the 21st Century Project began, remodeling the dressing rooms and second floor restroom was not originally in the plan. However it soon became apparent that the wallpaper and floor coverings were outdated next to how lovely everything else looked. The fundraising committee developed naming opportunities for various rooms. The auditorium became the Richmond Auditorium named after Lois and James Richmond. Frank Jamison purchased one of the dressing room naming opportunities in honor of his wife, Paula. She was the LLA president at the time of the dedication of the 21st Century Project and headed the fundraising aspect of the campaign.

The second dressing room was named after Naomi Stucki, a long-time actress at the Kalamazoo Civic Theatre, which sits directly across the alley from the LLA building. Her daughters, Marcia and Heidi, wished to honor their mother in a meaningful way. The view from the room window looks directly into the Civic Auditorium rehearsal room

where Naomi spent many hours. The daughters suggested that the room be decorated with an Art Deco glamour that fit the era of the 1931 addition. The powder room was also re-decorated and for the first time had both hot and cold running water.

❋ Bottom: Dressing rooms and donor plaques.

51

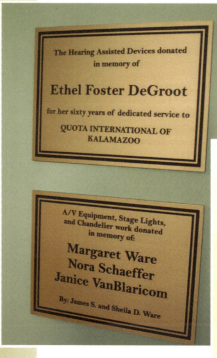
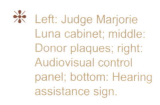

✻ Left: Judge Marjorie Luna cabinet; middle: Donor plaques; right: Audiovisual control panel; bottom: Hearing assistance sign.

One of the goals of the 21st Century Project was to increase the use of the auditorium by the public. Experts, such as Dr. D. Terry Williams of Western Michigan University's theatre department and Dr. Barry Ross, former concertmaster of the Kalamazoo Symphony Orchestra, gave advice on how to improve the acoustics. The heavy carpet and thick horsehair pad were removed, revealing beautiful original white pine floors. Paintings and wall hangings were placed elsewhere in the building. The side curtains were removed from the stage area.

In the hallway outside the auditorium, is a locked glass cabinet holding a judicial robe, gavel, and bench sign belonging to Judge Marjorie Luna. Her family donated these items to honor Judge Luna, who served as a judge of the Ninth District Court from 1970-1977. Judge Luna was the first female judge in Kalamazoo, appointed even though she did not have a law degree.

James and Sheila Ware, in honor of Margaret Ware, Nora Schaeffer, and Janice Van Blaricom donated state-of-the-art audiovisual equipment, stage lights, and chandelier work. Hearing assistance devices were given in memory of Ethel Foster DeGroot by her son Thomas DeGroot. In the past, the auditorium had been a magnet for cultural activities. For the 21st century, the auditorium is now ready for lectures, poetry readings, recitals, theatrical productions, meetings, and any other activities that fit the space.

※ Eastlake auditorium chairs.

Auditorium Chairs

The Eastlake-designed black walnut chairs with cane seats and backs were purchased with donated funds from Dr. and Mrs. Joseph Sill in 1883 (Potts and Lyons-Jenness 1997, 30). The 150 chairs were made in Grand Rapids, Michigan. Each chair cost $3.85 plus ten dollars shipping for a total cost of $577.50. They were originally too high for the ladies to sit comfortably as their feet did not touch the floor. The chair legs were then cut down and a brace was added to some to serve as a footrest for the lady seated behind. A few chairs of the original height remain. It has been noted that the chairs were rather uncomfortable for sitting for any length of time. Even so, the chairs added an historical elegance to the auditorium.

In 2015, it was decided that the Eastlake chairs were no longer practical. It became more difficult to find craft persons to repair the cane seats and backs. They squeaked and became a distraction during programs. Besides the discomfort of sitting for long periods of time in the chairs, the cane backs were rough on silks and other delicate fabrics worn by attendees. Funds to purchase 82 new chairs were donated by Lois and James Richmond. The chairs, which cost $238 each, are upholstered in red to match the stage curtains and have metal walnut wood-grain frames.

The old chairs in good condition were sold to members or interested community members.

Chandeliers

There have been many photographs published of the original chandeliers, both downstairs and upstairs. However, little has been written about them. During the 1974-1980 restoration, "The two large chandeliers were disassembled, stripped, scratch brushed, color buffed, and lacquered; reassembled, rewired, and rehung. New glass globes, which match the ones on the downstairs chandeliers, were installed. A very plain, bare chandelier nearest to the stage was removed and stored under the stage" (LLA Historical Restoration Program 1974-1980).

This chandelier was rediscovered under the stage during the 21st Century Project. It was bent and missing parts. Lois Richmond, President of the LLA at the time and chair of the construction committee, recalled seeing a box in the President's Room labeled "Missing Chandelier parts" and sure enough, they were the missing parts. The chandelier was picked up by Roger Parzyck of the Heritage Company, where it was cleaned and rewired. It was returned to the building and rehung over the stage.

✳ Bottom left: Ornate brass detail; top left: Cherub detail; top right: Cherub chandelier near stage.

✽ Top left: Greek runner chandelier near Park Street window; top right: Runner detail.

✽ Left: Broken chandelier (photo taken by Lisa Salay); middle: Storage area under stage where broken chandelier was discovered; right: Repaired, refurbished, and rehung stage chandelier.

Jim's Arch.

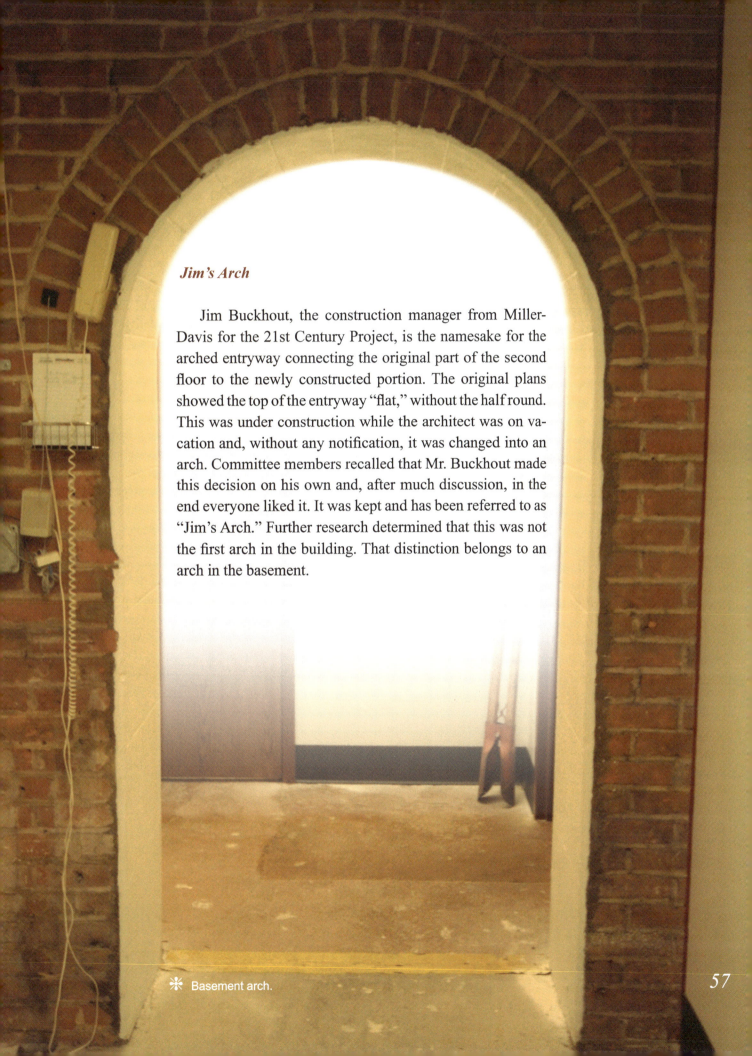

Jim's Arch

Jim Buckhout, the construction manager from Miller-Davis for the 21st Century Project, is the namesake for the arched entryway connecting the original part of the second floor to the newly constructed portion. The original plans showed the top of the entryway "flat," without the half round. This was under construction while the architect was on vacation and, without any notification, it was changed into an arch. Committee members recalled that Mr. Buckhout made this decision on his own and, after much discussion, in the end everyone liked it. It was kept and has been referred to as "Jim's Arch." Further research determined that this was not the first arch in the building. That distinction belongs to an arch in the basement.

✽ Basement arch.

✳ Top: Window lock; bottom left to right: Carved wooden stair railing; ornate sash lift on stage window; Victorian floral sash lock on stage window; mechanical window hardware remaining on main auditorium entry door; decorative floor heater grate; door hinges; and auditorium door pull.

Chapter 7
Times Past

"Keep all special thoughts and memories for lifetimes to come. Share these keepsakes with others to inspire hope and build from the past, which can bridge to the future."

-- Mattie Stepanek
(American poet)

Over the years, members of the Ladies' Library Association and various local publications have documented building changes, member and public celebrations, and community activities. Vintage photographs included in this book were discovered in various spaces within the LLA building, member collections, and Association archives held at the Charles C. and Lynn L. Zhang Legacy Collections Center at Western Michigan University. The oldest photos show the beautiful, elaborate Victorian interiors that the founding members surely created with pride. Carefully handwritten ledgers, kept since the inception of the Association, are invaluable in documenting the mission and work of this organization over the last 160 years.

✶ Archive photo of LLA exterior.

Top: Charles C. and Lynn L. Zhang Legacy Collections Center at Western Michigan University; middle: LLA file photo; bottom: Archive photo of LLA drama club performance.

✱ Early leather-bound LLA record book with excerpts of handwritten entries.

64

...Malvern. Mrs. McNair presented the name of Mrs. C. C. ... for us whom Chemistry Free... from Mrs. Downing, sent with the... the last meeting, but inadvertent... Mrs. Stone.

...M. A. Ford was made Hon. m... consideration to his hav... ing last year...

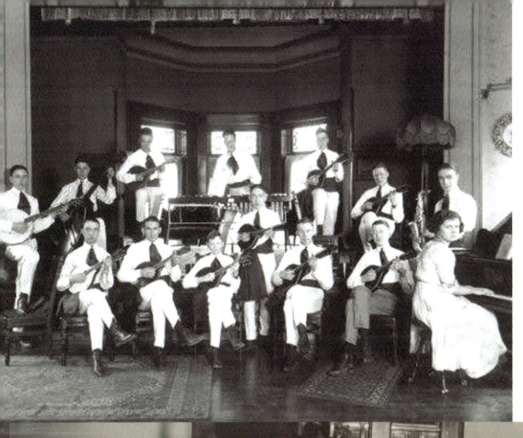

❋ Page 66: LLA file photo.
Page 67 top: Archive photo of mandolin orchestra performance; bottom: LLA file photo of auditorium.

67

Page 68-69: LLA file photo collage of member activities and programs.

Chapter 8
1931 Addition

"Love people. Cook them tasty food."
-- from a sign displayed in the current LLA kitchen

※ Vintage postcard featuring LLA building.

At the end of the Civil War, members of the Ladies' Library Association held "strawberry socials" to raise money to purchase additional books and artwork. During the following years many types of bake sales, ice cream socials, and teas were held to help fund a variety of projects. In 1918 and 1919, "cabaret teas" including musical performances became very popular, successful money makers. Members may have prepared refreshments for such events in their homes, as no kitchen existed at the time.

In 1919, in her last address to the Association, the president urged members to work for an addition to the building that included a new kitchen. At the LLA's first meeting of 1920, the Board resolved to raise money in the coming years to add to the building addition fund (Potts and Lyons-Jenness 1997, 68). Club activities of the mid-1920s demonstrated that the women were very serious about earning money for their new kitchen. They held food sales, club luncheons, bridge luncheons, and even Christmas card sales. Every penny went to their savings account at Fidelity Building and Loan Association, the only place the LLA invested its funds during this time prior to the stock market crash of 1929 (Potts and Lyons-Jenness 1997, 73).

Their determination is a testament to the vision of the LLA. Despite the ensuing Great Depression, by July of 1931, there was enough in the building fund to accept bids and "start the build-

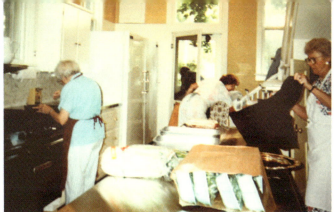

ing at once" (LLA Board of Directors Meeting Minutes 1931). The LLA awarded the contract to the O. F. Miller Construction Company (later known as the Miller-Davis Company) for $5,000. Plans included a two-story addition on the north side of the historic structure. The first floor would have a doorway to the foyer, a small lavatory, a kitchen, a rear entrance, and a staircase to the second floor. The second story included a doorway to the auditorium landing, a hallway, a small lavatory, two dressing rooms, and a storage room. This storage room evolved over the years to become the President's Room and became a mini-archive of LLA documents. For that reason, it is always kept locked.

During construction the group rented a meeting room from the Kalamazoo Civic Theatre for $120 and held food sales to pay that expense. By December, they made their final payment to the contractor and had enough money to buy a new oil furnace (Potts and Lyons-Jenness 1997, 74)!

During the Depression, the ladies put the kitchen to good use in spite of the rising cost of food and poor attendance. They invited various women's clubs to hold meetings at the LLA, now that there was a new, convenient kitchen for food preparation. Later in 1947, a grant from the Kalamazoo Foundation allowed the purchase of a new stove, a new refrigerator, and cooking utensils. Cooking activities increased and in the fall of 1949 the *Cooky Book* was sold at the club bazaar for sixty cents (Potts and Lyons-Jenness 1997, 83-85).

In the 1980s, the Ways & Means Committee began to prepare and serve food for members and public events under the leadership of Betty Wolbers. These events increased the visibility of the LLA in the community. They published three additional cookbooks in 1998, 2004, and 2010 with recipes frequently served at their events. A few favorite recipes are included here from the 2010 *Ladies' Library Cookbook*.

✻ Top left clockwise: Originally a stained-glass window, converted to kitchen doorway, and later sealed in 21st Century building project; LLA file photo of 1930s kitchen addition; hallway and dressing room entrances; small upstairs lavatory; storage room that currently serves as the Presidents' Room; and three published LLA cookbooks.

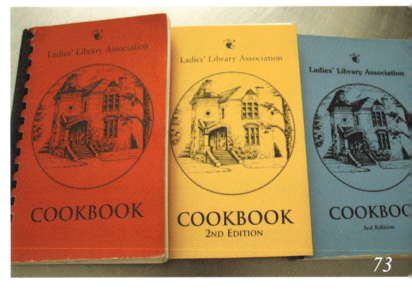

Refrigerator Yeast Dough (used for Cinnamon, Parmesan, and Herb Rolls)

2 pkgs. dry yeast
½ cup sugar
1 Tbsp. salt
7-½ cups flour, divided
1 egg
½ cup butter, melted

Dissolve 2 packages dry yeast in ½ cup warm water. In a large bowl, dissolve ½ cup sugar and 1 tablespoon of salt in 2 cups warm water. Add yeast mixture. Add 4 cups flour and stir vigorously. Add egg and melted butter (not hot); stir well. Add remaining 3-½ cups flour. Dough will be stiff. Cover well with plastic wrap or put in large plastic container with lid. Be sure bowl is large enough as dough will rise in the refrigerator. The next day or within a week, remove from refrigerator and shape into rolls. Allow to double in size. This takes approximately 2 hours. Bake at 375 degrees. Makes 32 to 40 rolls. Add cinnamon, Parmesan cheese or herbs of choice during final shaping.

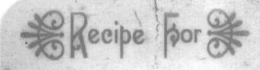

Parmesan Pita Wedges

4 pita bread rounds
1 cup finely grated Parmesan cheese
½ cup mayonnaise
½ tsp. oregano
½ tsp. basil
½ tsp. garlic powder
1 tsp. Worcestershire sauce

Mix all ingredients for topping. Spread on pita bread. Cut each into 8 triangles with pizza cutter. Bake on parchment paper for 15 minutes at 350 degrees. Makes 32.

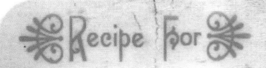 **Chicken with Apricot Glaze**

8 boneless, skinless chicken breast halves

Sauce:

1 cup apricot preserves

½ cup Russian dressing

1 tsp. paprika

4 Tbsp. dry onion soup mix

2 Tbsp. flour

¼ cup water

Place chicken breast halves in greased baking pan. Mix apricot preserves, Russian dressing, paprika, dry onion soup mix, water, and flour. Pour over chicken breasts. Cover pan with foil and bake 45 minutes in 350 degree oven. Remove foil and bake 15 minutes more. Serve with rice to which you have added crushed pineapple and raisins or cranberries.

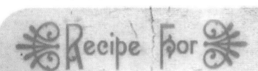 **Toffee Bars**

2 pkgs. graham crackers

1 cup butter melted

1 cup brown sugar, packed

1 cup pecans, chopped

Line an 11x17-inch pan with a single layer of graham crackers. Stir butter, brown sugar and nuts together in medium saucepan and cook over medium heat until sugar dissolves. Spread evenly over the crackers. Bake at 375 degrees for 15 minutes. Do not burn. Cut apart immediately.
Makes at least 36 bars.

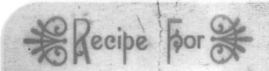 ## Strawberry Spinach Salad

5 cups spinach leaves, cleaned and torn

2 cups lettuce, cleaned and torn

½ cup celery, sliced

1 cup green grapes, halved

2 cups strawberries, washed, hulled and sliced

Chill. Just before serving pour 1 cup dressing over and toss. Serves 8.

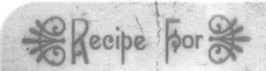 ## Raspberry Dressing

1 cup red wine vinegar

1-½ cup sugar

1 cup salad oil

12 oz. raspberry concentrate, thawed

½ tsp. dried basil

Mix well and refrigerate. This dressing recipe makes more than enough for 8 servings.

Refrigerate remaining dressing.

Members of the Ladies' Library take pride in the appearance and presentation of the food and beverages they serve. The tradition of using silver tea sets, silver coffee servers, and glass punch bowls at monthly teas continues. These items and accessory pieces help to establish a Victorian-era atmosphere in the historic building. The china table service and crystal used for all events may have changed over the years, but each formal, complete place setting adds to the total experience for guests. Engravings on the coffee and tea service pieces document long years of service by members and recognition by various community organizations. Several large silver loving cups denote clubwomen and musical achievements. The past presidents of LLA presented one of the coffee servers, while two others were given to commemorate long-time members.

❋ Top: LLA signature china; middle: Silver display cabinet in main library room; bottom right: Crystal stemware; bottom left: China and flatware

✽ Coffee urn presented to the membership by the past presidents.

❋ Top: A preserved LLA program; middle: Coffee server donated by the family of Florence G. Mills in memory of her 47 year LLA membership; bottom left: Engraved loving cups; bottom right: Engraved silver serving pieces.

Chapter 9 *Statuary*

"The sculpture is already complete within the marble block, before I start my work. It is already there, I just have to chisel away the superfluous material."

-- Michelangelo Buonarroti (Italian sculpture and artist)

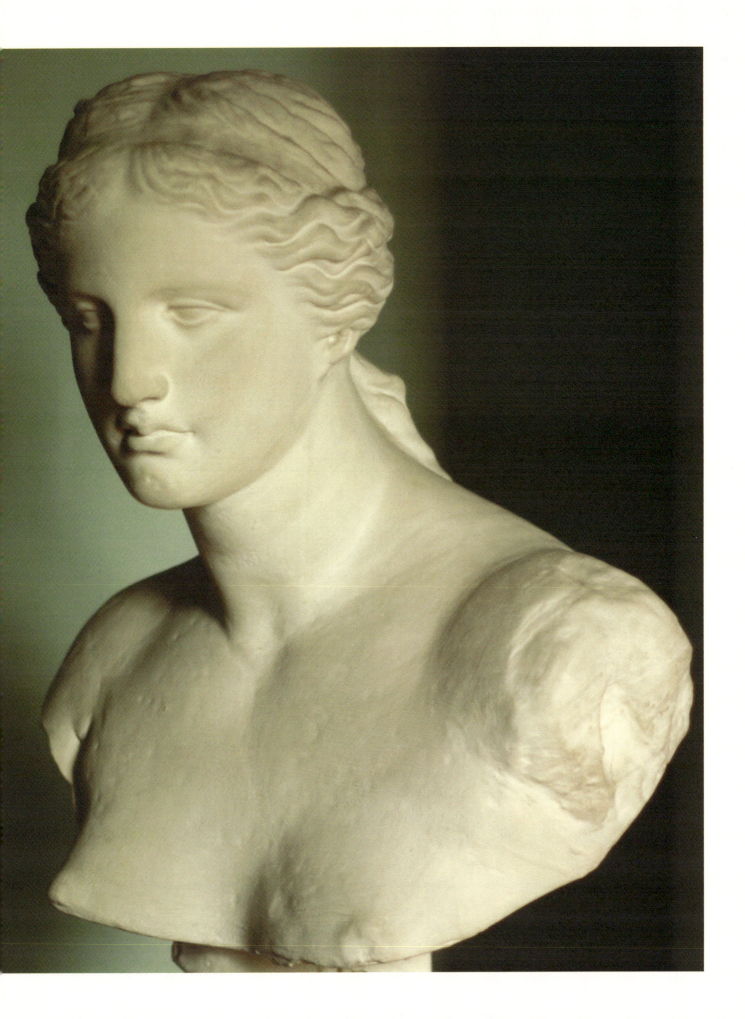

✱ *Psyche.*

Sculptures

Several of the earliest photos of the interior of the LLA building show four plaster casts of Greek and Roman sculptures. Lucinda Hinsdale Stone purchased these busts in Paris. Plaster casts copied from the ancient marble Greek and Roman busts were standard fare in the 19th century. They were found in art schools, smaller museums and institutions of learning, and even private homes of middle class and well-to-do families (Sheridan 2002). Many of the early members of the LLA studied the Greek antiquities under the instruction of Lucinda who had a special interest in Greek history (Potts and Lyons-Jenness 1997, 21).

The first statue depicts *Psyche*, goddess of the soul. In Greek mythology, Psyche's astounding beauty earned the ire of Aphrodite who forced Psyche to perform a series of labors in order to find her lost love Cupid. Another bust is of *Apollo Belvedere*, the great Olympian god of prophecy and oracles, healing, music, song and poetry, and the protection of the young. The third bust represents *Venus,* goddess of love and beauty, and mother of Cupid (Theoi Greek Mythology 2011).

These figures from Greek mythology are fairly well known, but the fourth bust is less familiar, that of *Antinous*, a favorite of the Roman Emperor Hadrian in the second century. For the LLA's 25th anniversary in 1877, member Mrs. G. H. Mason wrote a poem that highlighted some of the artwork in the building. Of Antinous she wrote: "That is young Antoninus [*sic*] the beautiful friend / Of the Emperor Hadrian, whose tragic end / He so mourned, and no art could his sorrow beguile / Since the fair Antoninus was drowned in the Nile" (Potts and Lyons-Jenness 1997, 25). Hadrian deified Antinous after his tragic death and commissioned many sculptures and coins of him. Many of these have survived and they depict Antinous as a model of youthful beauty (Antinous 2010). Lucinda may have imparted these ideas to her students in courses that she taught at the LLA.

✳ Top left clockwise: *Apollo Belvedere*; *Venus*; and *Antinous*.

❋ Union Refugees.

❋ The Home Guard–Midnight on the Border.

❋ Taking the Oath and Drawing Rations.

Rogers Groups

The LLA collection also includes six sculptures called Rogers Groups named for the American sculptor John Rogers (1829-1904).

These statues were the perfect size for plush Victorian parlors with bay windows and marble-topped tables. Indeed, John Rogers created popular, affordable art that became a nationwide vogue. Rogers developed a flexible mold that allowed mass-production and, therefore, an average selling price of $14. Rogers popularity once rivaled that of Currier and Ives. His groups were most desirable during the 1870s and 1880s, a time when the Civil War was still fresh in the minds of nearly every family (Sheridan 2002).

Four of the six groupings depict Civil War themes. *Union Refugees* (1863) represents a Union family that must flee their home in the South. The father carries all they can take in a bundle on his gun, while the son consoles his mother with flowers. The LLA purchased this group with funds raised from a successful Valentine's Day party in February 1872 (LLA Board of Directors Meeting Minutes 1872). *The Home Guard–Midnight on the Border* (1865) shows two young women left alone to guard the home as the men serve in the army. The older woman cocks her revolver as the younger girl clings to her for protection. *Taking The Oath and Drawing Rations* (1865) depicts a scene after the war when many Southern families were very much reduced in means and obliged to ask for food from the government. A Southern lady, with her son at her side, reluctantly takes an

❋ Abraham Lincoln and the Council of War, hand detail.

❋ Abraham Lincoln and the Council of War.

oath of allegiance in order to draw rations from a Union officer.

In *Abraham Lincoln and the Council of War* (1868) the subjects are Lincoln, General Ulysses S. Grant, and Secretary of War Edwin M. Stanton. Lincoln reviews Grant's strategies for the Civil War campaign of 1864 as Grant and Stanton look on. Lincoln's son, Robert Todd Lincoln, is reported to have said that this was the best likeness of his father he had ever seen (Sheridan 2002). This grouping was a donation in January 1872 by

84

  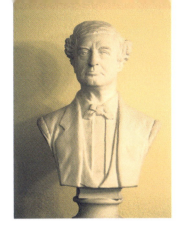 

member Mrs. Alfred Wortley (LLA Board of Directors Meeting Minutes 1872).

John Rogers made several versions of *Abraham Lincoln and the Council of War*. All versions involve changes in Stanton's hands: in the first, Stanton is cleaning his glasses behind Lincoln's head; in the second, Stanton's hands are empty at his waist; and in the third, Stanton's hands are moved forward of Lincoln's head. Historians can only speculate why these versions were made, but some collectors suggest that Rogers was influenced by prospective buyers who questioned the possibility of Stanton's involvement in Lincoln's assassination and who, therefore, might not buy the sculpture with Stanton doing anything with his hands behind the head of the beloved President (Bleier 1976, 78). The LLA owns the second version of this group with Stanton's hands empty.

Two more Rogers groups complete the LLA collection. *Coming to the Parson* (1870) portrays a shy young couple approaching the minister to make their marriage plans. The most commercially successful for Rogers, this group was popular as a wedding gift and drew sales numbering at 8,000 (Bleier 1976, 84). The Reverend Wayne Conner, the youth pastor of the Kalamazoo First Presbyterian Church donated this sculpture to the LLA in 2009. Finally, *The School Examination* (1867) depicts a young schoolgirl reciting for a visiting member of the school board while the teacher looks on, anxious about the performance of her pupil.

Two smaller statues are on the shelves of the lending library room. One is of William Jennings Bryan and the other, Daniel Webster. Most likely members donated these statues.

Barry Bauman of the Chicago Conservation Center cleaned the sculptures (and the paintings) in 1992. This unique statuary collection has contributed significantly to the Victorian atmosphere of the building.

Great American Women Figurine Doll Collection

In the new second floor hallway are two small wood display cabinets holding 24 "statuettes." Each doll is six-inches tall and originally cost $49. These detailed images include First Ladies from Martha Washington to Jacqueline Kennedy, as well as other notable women like Clara Barton, Pocahontas, and Princess Diana.

They are from the Great American Women Figurine Doll Collection of "half dolls" issued by the United States Historical Society. Half dolls were originally used on ladies' dressing tables as pincushions. Later some covered powder and hair dishes, while others became lamps or jewelry holders. The set was collected by member Barbara Baker and donated to the LLA in 2013. Today the display fascinates many visitors of all ages.

✳ Top left to right: *Coming to the Parson*; *The School Examination*; bust of William Jennings Bryan; and small statue of Daniel Webster. Middle right: Great American Doll Figurines.

Chapter 10
Stained Glass

"Let there be many windows to your soul, that all the glory of the universe may beautify it."

-- Ella Wheeler Wilcox (stated by Lucinda Hinsdale Stone to be her favorite verse)

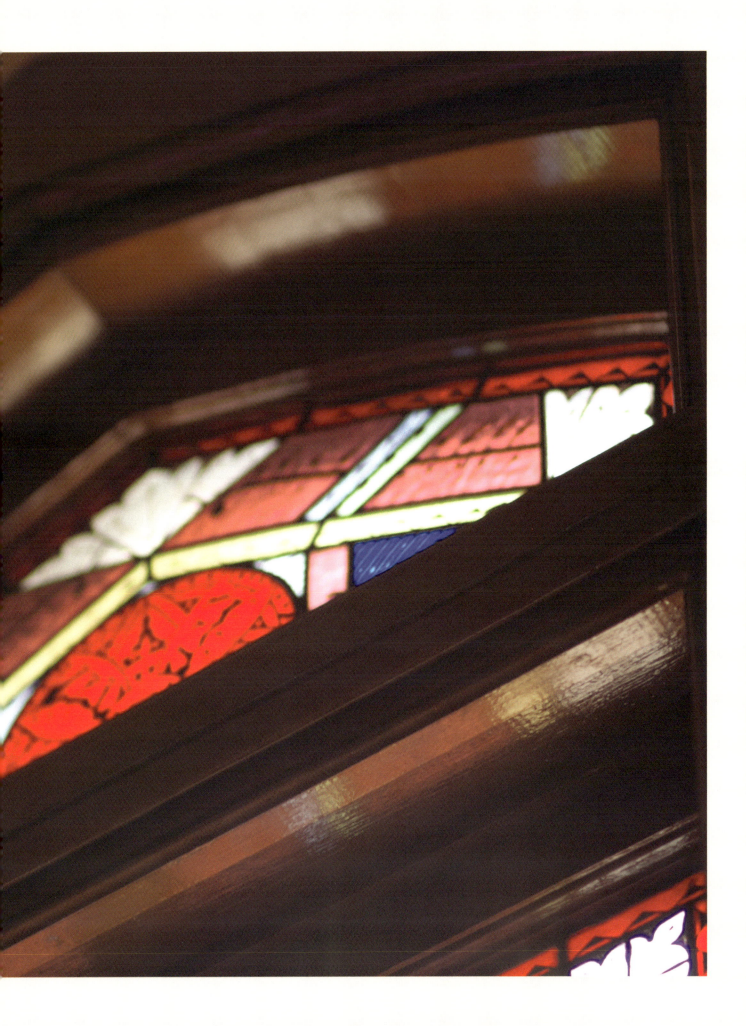

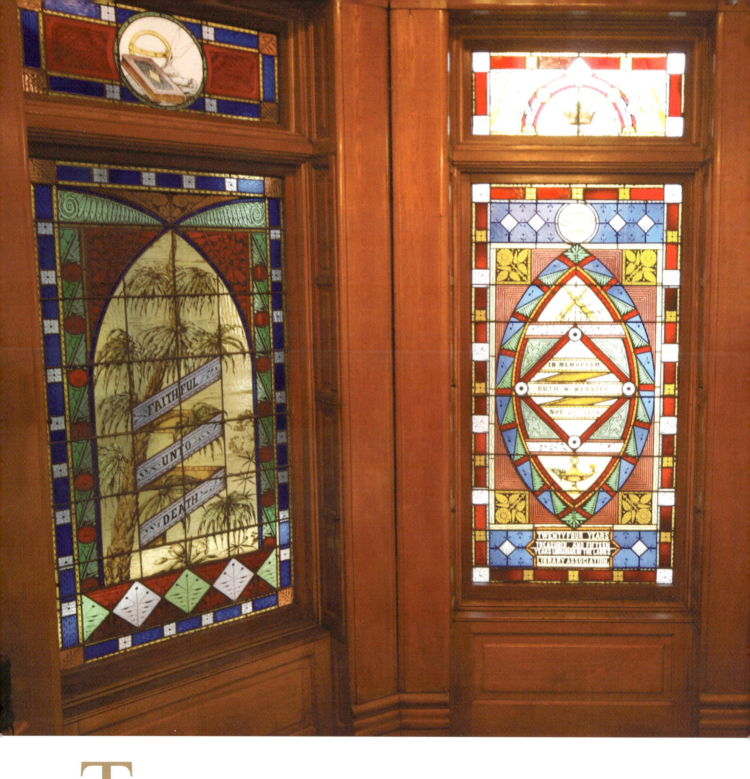

The most striking feature of the library building may be the stained glass, both the vintage and the modern. Building plans of 1878 included 14 literary-themed transoms that not only were decorative, but also functional, providing ventilation for the building. The Ruth Webster Memorial Window was planned shortly after her death in November of 1878. The minutes of 1879 indicate that two payments, one of $566.25 and another of $75, were made to the W. H. Wells & Bros. Glass Company of Chicago. In 2002, an impressive modern window was commissioned to commemorate the building's 150th anniversary.

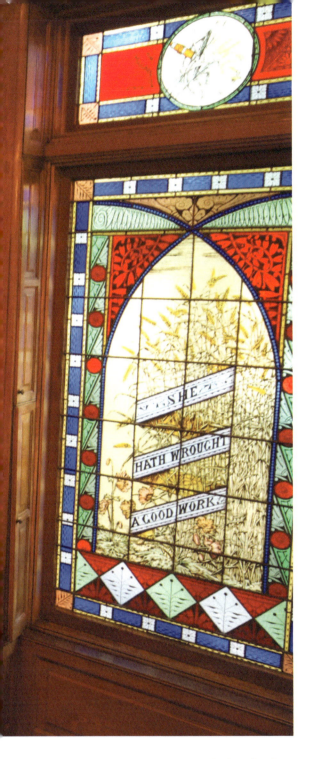

Ruth Webster Memorial Window

The bay window on the east end of the main library room was chosen as the best place for the memorial window to honor Mrs. Webster. An unidentified English artist associated with the Wells Company designed and executed the window consisting of three almost-equal parts. It reflects a Moorish style that was experiencing a revival of interest in the middle to late 1800s. In that style, no human images are included. This window, therefore, includes images and symbols that epitomize the life, faith, and work of Ruth Webster. Above the central feminine shape are two inverted torches emblematic of death, and below the same is a burning lamp, emblematic of life. The lower portion contains the words "Twenty-four years treasurer and fifteen years librarian of the Ladies' Library Association." The left hand panel contains other religious symbols of the palm tree, the lily, and a stalk of golden fleece. The right section is filled with ripe wheat and poppies, which tell of a life of good works and the final sleep of death. The motto here is, "She hath wrought a good work." The upper medallions show a globe, a book, and an inkstand with pens on the left; and on the right, a sickle and a handful of gathered grain. The border on either side is conventionalized palms and roses of Sharon (den Bleyker 1906).

Ruth Webster died before she ever saw this beautiful tribute and the completed building to which she devoted much effort. Her efforts were not lost on Lucinda Stone, who called Webster a "social evolutionist" because of the changes and improvements Webster brought to the Association (*Kalamazoo Daily Telegraph* 1895).

Lines of Knowledge

The beautiful modern window that faces Park Street was conceived in 2002 as a project to celebrate the 150th anniversary of the Association (in 1852). Under the direction of then-President Shirley Shane and Grounds Chair Dorothy Dykema, the planning committee funded the project with a bequest from Fern and Herbert Rodewald. They commissioned stained-glass artist Jamie Rife, a high school art teacher, to do the work. His completed design *Lines of Knowledge* was installed on May 6, 2003. Rife's work currently appears at the Kalamazoo Public Library, the Park Club, the United Methodist Church of Kalamazoo, and Bell's Brewery.

Throughout the windows, a series of long, flowing lines in opalescent glass emerge from the book at the lower left and continue through the three panels on a diagonal to the upper right. These, according to Rife, represent the *Lines of Knowledge* that have their origin in books and the cultural life that the LLA has fostered since its inception. Details within the windows represent the various ways in which the LLA has traditionally contributed to the community and continues to do so today.

Specifically, on the left a group of children seated in front of their teacher represents the many educational programs supported by the LLA, particularly in outreach to the young. In the center panel, a vignette of a city represents Kalamazoo, the locus of the majority of LLA activities. Also in the center is a table supporting a vase of yellow roses, the official flower of the LLA. The third panel features a violin and musical staff representing the fine arts and cultural activities promoted by the Association. The plate of sweets, the china cup, and the saucer symbolize the hospitality that is an essential part of the LLA tradition. The third panel also features an open book with cursive words, to indicate that the story of the LLA is still being written.

A number of small, colorful spheres appear throughout each of the three panels. These faceted "jewels" cast a spectrum when direct sunlight hits them, creating a pleasing visual effect. There are also clear ones that are optical, which, when looked into, cause things to appear upside down (Rife 2015). These jewels were provided by additional donations from many of the members. A framed list of the donors is displayed alongside the window.

At one point in the design process, Rife submitted plans for the right-hand panel to include a straight-sided coffee mug by the plate of sweets. Betty Wolbers voiced the fact that the LLA never uses mugs for their events, but instead uses the handsome LLA china service. Rife accordingly changed the design. Also during the construction of the windows, the window planning committee visited the Rife studio. Rife invited the ladies to create some of the final cuttings. Mary Jane Kreidler, Dorothy Dykema, Shirley Shane, and the late Betty Wolbers cut the corner amber pieces for the center window. Rife consciously chose colors that would harmonize with the older stained glass and even included some vintage glass in the construction. His design effectively represents the history and mission of the Ladies' Library, and it also is a true reflection of the state of stained-glass artistry in the early 21st century (LLA Docent Handbook 2014).

❋ Left: Faceted "jewels" in window; right: detail depicting LLA hospitality.

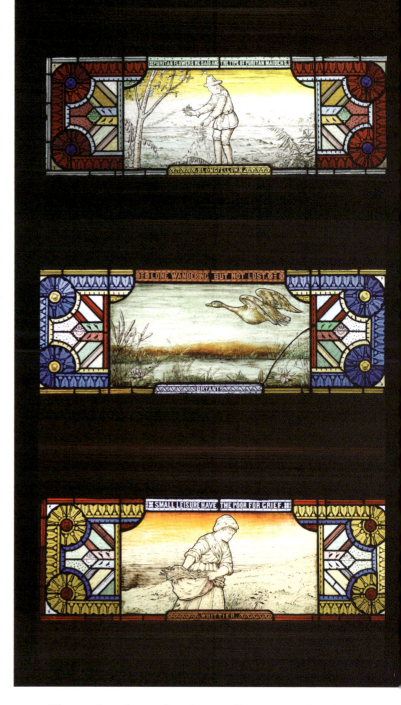

✻ Top to bottom: "The Courtship Of Miles Standish" by Henry Wadsworth Longfellow; "To a Waterfowl" by William Cullen Bryant; and "Mable Martin: A Harvest Idyl" by John Greenleaf Whittier.

The Literary Transoms

The transom windows, which reflect literary works and figures, truly make the building unique. Long-time Director of Collections and Exhibitions of the Kalamazoo Institute of Arts, the late Helen Sheridan wrote a detailed description of these transoms. She wrote, the transoms "serve as a beautiful, decorative shield between the outer world and the safe, protected environment within the building. They enhance this interior environment with the glowing light of their pure colors, and they reinforce the awareness that we are in a very special place" (Sheridan 2002). These transoms do indeed make the building a very special place, just as the founding members intended.

For an 1890 magazine article, Caroline Stanley, a Kalamazoo schoolteacher and member of the LLA, wrote: "These windows were the subject of much thought by the ladies. First, representative authors were selected; then illustrations were hunted up, and appropriate quotations found. These were given to the designer to be worked out. If satisfactory, they were approved; if not, they were returned and others substituted" (Stanley 1890). The resultant selections not only reflect a desire to represent significant works of literature, but also serve as instruments in the moral education of the community, a mission supported by the Association whole-heartedly (Sheridan 2002).

Each transom includes side panels in a stained-glass pattern and a center panel that is a painted illustration from the chosen literary work of an author. Above the illustration is a quote from the work. The main library room contains four of the transoms. First, from Henry Wadsworth Longfellow's work "The Courtship of Miles Standish," John Alden is shown gathering flowers that he will present to his love, Priscilla Mullins, on behalf of his friend, the blunt old Captain Miles Standish. The quote "Puritan flowers, he said, and the type of Puritan Maidens" shows Alden's admiration for the young Priscilla. In spite of Alden's loyalty to Standish, Priscilla eventually tells Alden to

✳ Top to bottom: ""Rip Van Winkle" by Washington Irving; *Aurora Leigh* by Elizabeth Barrett Browning; and portraits of Novella D'Andrea (left) and Clotilde Tambroni (right).

the south wall. In "Mabel Martin," Whittier tells a story set in the aftermath of the notorious Salem witch trials. "Small leisure have the poor for grief" refers to the fact that since Mabel's mother has been accused and hanged as a witch, Mabel has no time to mourn and must find courage to keep at her spinning wheel if she is to make her own way in the world.

The fourth transom sits above the kitchen doorway and pictures old Rip from Washington Irving's "Rip Van Winkle." Rip wakes after his 20-year sleep and says: "My very dog has forgotten me." Always looking to avoid work and his wife, Rip has slept through perhaps the best part of his life—including the Revolutionary War. However, his daughter, now grown with her own family, recognizes him and brings him home.

The only woman author represented in the transoms is Elizabeth Barrett Browning. This window is above the *Lines of Knowledge* window in the lending library. Browning's illustration is the center panel in what is called *The Women's Window*. Her long novel / poem *Aurora Leigh,* published in 1856, made Browning a major figure in Victorian literature. Below the quotation "Aurora Leigh, the earliest of aurora's [*sic*]," the illustration shows Aurora meeting her beau who greets her with those words. Aurora, well educated through her own efforts, is a model for 19th century women.

Flanking Browning's transom are portraits in glass of two "learned women of Bologna" that

speak for himself and the young lovers do come together.

Next, William Cullen Bryant's "To a Waterfowl" shows a lone goose, perhaps cut off from its fellows but who will instinctively find its way home. "Lone wandering, but not lost…" suggests that a sound moral and spiritual training of the young will help to safely see them through the trials of life that will surely come.

John Greenleaf Whittier's "Mable Martin: A Harvest Idyl" is the third in the triumvirate of 19th century American poet-storytellers represented on

93

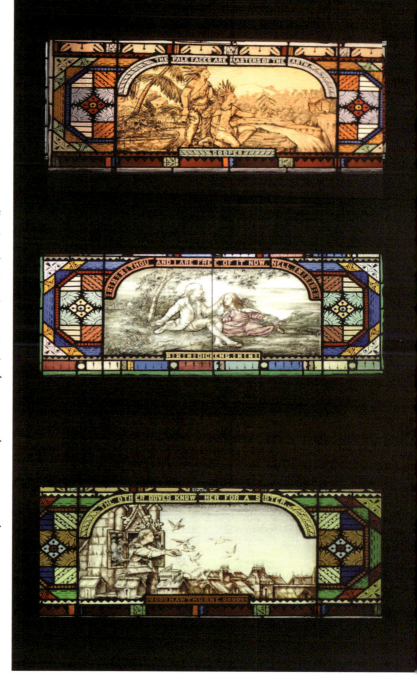

✻ Top to bottom: *The Last of the Mohicans: A Narrative of 1757* by James Fenimore Cooper; *The Old Curiosity Shop* by Charles Dickens; and *The Marble Faun* by Nathaniel Hawthorne.

complete *The Women's Window*. On the left is Novella D'Andrea who was admitted to the University of Bologna as a teaching chair in the 14th century. Daughter of a distinguished lawyer, she often stepped in for her father and gave his lectures. Later she lectured on philosophy and law, but from behind a curtain, so her beauty would not distract the attention of her (male) students (Bolton 1881). She is one of five "learned women of Bologna" honored in that city. On the right of Browning is another, Clotilde Tambroni (Matilda in some sources). Tambroni was professor of Greek and Greek literature from 1793 to 1808 at the University of Bologna. Apparently, the institution included women on the faculty early on (Agnew 1868).

Upstairs on the stage in the Richmond Auditorium, three transoms pay tribute to classic literature by Cooper, Dickens, and Hawthorne. The first is of James Fenimore Cooper's historical novel *The Last of the Mohicans: A Narrative of 1757* published in 1826. The quotation "The palefaces are masters of the Earth" would hopefully be interpreted today more sympathetically to Native Americans. The illustration shows Mohican warriors looking across a river at a mill and house of a white settler, symbols of the "improving" effects of (white) civilization. The transom for Charles Dickens depicts a scene from *The Old Curiosity Shop* where Little Nell and her grandfather rest under a tree in the countryside. He says to her "Thou and I are free of it now, Nell…" The quote refers to the misery of the city and the cruel people there to whom he has lost his shop, a common occurrence of the Industrial Revolution in London of that time. The last transom on the stage honors Nathaniel Hawthorne and depicts a scene from *The Marble Faun*, his romantic mystery set in Italy. The quote "The other doves know her for a sister" refers to the character of Hilda who represents innocence throughout the novel. This novel, with its many descriptions of historic sites, served somewhat as a travel guide to Lucinda Stone as she

✷ Top to bottom: *The Deserted Village* by Oliver Goldsmith; "Lancelot and Elaine" by Alfred, Lord Tennyson; and "Tam o"Shanter" by Robert Burns

toured Rome, Italy, with young women students (Perry 1902, 70).

In addition to Dickens on the stage, six other European authors are represented on the remaining transoms. On the south wall of the auditorium, the first transom shows Irish poet Oliver Goldsmith's *The Deserted Village*, a long poem that condemns rural depopulation and greed. "Children followed, with endearing wile…" refers to the fact that the preacher has a strong influence on the moral upbringing of the children of a village that has been deserted by many of the working-aged men. The second transom quotes Alfred, Lord Tennyson's poem titled, "Lancelot and Elaine," part of his larger work *Idylls of the King*. Elaine is pictured on her funeral bier floating down a river, "In her right hand the lily, in her left the letter." The letter reveals to the kingdom her unrequited love for Lancelot and his cruelty to her. Third is a scene from Robert Burns' "Tam o'Shanter." The Scot describes one of the folktales of his native Ayr in western Scotland. In this tale, Tam stays too long at the market and must return home near midnight, riding past an abandoned church. The churchyard is known as a meeting place for witches and devilry. Tam sees his neighbors dancing there, among them a lady wearing a very short frock, exposing a private part of her anatomy. Tam laughs out loud and is immediately set upon by witches. He heads his horse for a nearby bridge, because "A running stream they dare na cross."

The transoms on the west wall of the auditorium honor three seminal figures in the visual and literary arts: William Shakespeare, Michelangelo, and Dante. The center panel shows Cordelia at the bedside of her father King Lear. In Shakespeare's tragedy *King Lear*, Lear has been mistreated by his other daughters and is left to wander all night on the moors during a storm. Cordelia, the only daughter to truly love and honor her father, attends to him. She ponders, "Is this a face to be opposed against the jarring winds…?" The left panel is a portrait of Michelangelo and the right panel is a portrait of Dante.

The final transom in the auditorium depicts

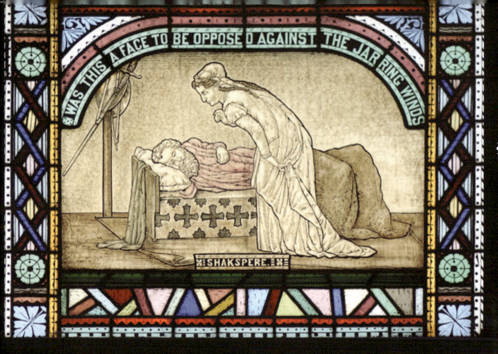

Left: *King Lear* by William Shakespeare; right: Portrait of Michelangelo.

John Milton and a quote from his essay "On His Blindness." The window here describes the blind Milton, dictating passages from *Paradise Lost* to one of his daughters, while another stands attentively listening. The quote "they also serve who only stand and wait" argues for patience and courage when confronted with adversity. In Milton's case, his blindness and inability to lead an active physical life did not prevent him from creating one of the greatest literary masterworks in the English language (Sheridan 2002).

Historical descriptions of the windows include a reference to yet another window, Goethe's *Faust* pictured in his library, with the quote: "Here I stand with my lore, poor fool, no wiser than before." This transom does not exist today, but was possibly above the doorway next to the stage leading to the hallway that was added in 1931 (den Bleyker 1906). It was lost, perhaps in that construction or some time later.

In 1996, these wonderful windows became part of the Michigan Stained Glass Census that is maintained in a computerized archive at the Michigan State University Museum. Herman Dykema, husband of then-Grounds Chair Dorothy Dykema, was largely responsible for photographing and describing these windows and completing the necessary forms so that the windows could be entered into the database, a valuable documentation for the study and appreciation of stained glass in Michigan institutions and communities. After the new window was completed in 2003, Mr. Dykema completed the process again for *Lines of Knowledge*, so those windows could be included in the Census (H. Dykema 1996).

✱ Left: Portrait of Dante; right: *Paradise Lost* by John Milton.

The stained-glass windows are a special part of the "personality" of the building and maintenance of them has always been important. Originally part of the restoration plans in the 1970s, protecting the windows with Lexan panels on the exterior was finally achieved in 2003-2004. However, the Lexan panels were removed during the 21st Century Project as they were found to be advancing the deterioration of the windows. Also, the first-floor windows of the new addition of 2013 were designed with transoms, for the possibility of more stained glass in the future.

Chapter 11
Paintings and Wall Hangings

"See these beautiful parlors, embellished by Art,
Each object before us designed to impart
A love for the beautiful, or to convey
Some lessons or thought in a most charming way..."
-- Mrs. G. H. Mason
(LLA member, 1877)

The Victorian ladies who founded the LLA came to Michigan mainly from New York State and New England, an area of the new nation that had quickly established educational and cultural institutions. Women like Lucinda Stone and Ruth Webster knew that they must recreate—for themselves and the community—the culture and civilities that they had left behind. This included art. As early as 1869, the LLA minutes refer to a "picture and statuary" fund to purchase works that would create an interest and appreciation of art for Kalamazoo citizens (Potts and Lyons-Jenness 1997, 16).

The collection is due primarily to Lucinda Stone who began purchasing works in Florence, Italy, and a few in London and Paris. Stone traveled to Europe with students on study abroad trips that she organized, the first travel opportunities for Kalamazoo College women.

The LLA possessed many items before they ever had their own building. "The two rooms in Fireman's Hall seemed to be almost overflowing with pictures, books, statuary and display cabinets..." (Potts and Lyons-Jenness 1997, 22). Several of the works were painted by, or are depictions of, strong, admirable women. The fund for these paintings was collected, in part, by the "tuition" paid by students in Mrs. Stone's 20-week classes on Greek history and art, and the well-attended drawing classes by Mrs. John Cadman (Potts and Lyons-Jenness 1997, 21).

Early Major Acquisitions

The largest and two most impressive paintings (both purchased in 1872) are *Self-Portrait* by Marie Louise Vigeé LeBrun, now in the main library room, and *Dante and Beatrice*, located upstairs in the new foyer. The LLA's August 1872 article in the daily newspaper announced the "safe arrival" of these paintings:

> One is a fine copy of Ary Scheffer's "Dante and Beatrice," of which there exists, at present, two originals. One is in the Boston Athenaeum, one of its chief art treasures; the other, painted by the artist under the patronage of Louis Philippe, is in the gallery of the Luxembourg in Paris. Kalamazoo is now in possession of an exquisite copy, from the studio of Professor Anthony Sasso and Son, of Florence. The other painting today added to the collection…is a beautiful copy of the celebrated portrait of Madame LeBrun, one of the most admired paintings of the Uffizi Gallery in Florence (L. H. Stone, "Fine Arts in Kalamazoo" 1872).

✼ *Dante and Beatrice* by Ary Scheffer.

The Dutch-French Romantic painter Ary Scheffer (1795-1858) completed the original *Dante l'Beatrice* in 1846. He often painted subjects from literature, especially the works of Dante, Byron, and Goethe. This large painting portrays Dante Alighieri (1265-1321), poet and author of the allegorical poem *The Divine Comedy*. The painting also shows Beatrice, who guides Dante through Paradise. In *The Divine Comedy*, Dante created one of the most celebrated fictionalized women in literature. He based his character on Beatrice Portinari, a Florentine woman with whom Dante claimed to have fallen in love at first sight—although he never really knew her well (Dante Alighieri 2010).

A month after the arrival of these paintings, Lucinda Stone wrote another article for the newspaper describing the subject of the self-portrait, Marie Louise Elizabeth Vigeé LeBrun, one of a very few

101

Self Portrait by Marie Louise Elizabeth Vigeé LeBrun.

women artists to make a successful career in painting. Known as Madame LeBrun, she was born in Paris in 1755, the daughter of a skillful portrait painter. Her father recognized her talents when she was very young and he encouraged her to develop her skills. He introduced her to fine teachers of the French Academy. At age 13, Marie and her mother were left in poverty when her father died. Her mother remarried, this time to a self-indulgent, greedy man, who later took control of Marie's income from her success.

Her finances did not improve with her own marriage. At 16, she married Jean LeBrun, a painter and art dealer with his own self-indulgences and vices. In spite of being exploited, she was happy in her career. She became a favorite of the French royal family and a friend to Marie Antoinette. During the French Revolution, Madame LeBrun fled to Italy where she was warmly welcomed by various academies of art. She continued her painting career, even when she was well into her eighties. In her autobiography, she wrote that she had completed 662 portraits (L. H. Stone 1872).

Self Portrait is an impressive painting. The young Marie stands at her easel—palette in hand—with a cheerful expression and a large hat atop her head, working on a portrait of Marie Antoinette. In 1872, Lucinda purchased this copy in Florence for $100.

Perhaps some citizens (and maybe even some LLA members) wondered why the LLA would deviate from books to art, especially in such a grand way. Lucinda answered their questions with this inspiring response:

> …is there not in the life of a woman like Madame LeBrun, whose portrait will now ever be open to the study of those who go to the library for books, a lesson as important and instructive as can be drawn from any book? Is there not in the industry and the perseverance of such a character—her wonderful achievements under possible discouragement, and the preservation of her powers through their continued use to such an advanced age—is there not life lessons as well as art lessons, that make this picture alone, worth more than it cost to place it—certainly a thing of beauty—before our children, as a weekly study and reminder of what may be endured and what achieved when the heart and mind together are set upon achievement (L. H. Stone 1872)?

104

✳ Left: *The Sybil of the Capitol* by Caroline Moore Stone; right: *Portrait of Vittoria Colonna* also by Caroline Moore Stone.

Additional Paintings

Another fine portrait on display is *The Sybil of the Capitol.* The figure is based on one of Michelangelo's Sybil images in the Sistine Chapel. Sybils were mysterious figures reputed to possess powers of prophecy, foretelling the future, or communicating messages. The figure's face is heavily shadowed to create an air of mystery. A *Kalamazoo Gazette* article in 1883 reported the acquisition of this painting: "Mrs. Stone has generously given four lectures upon art subjects, which were highly prized, and the proceeds from them have by agreement been paid toward the purchase of a beautiful picture 'The Sybil of the Capitol' painted by Mrs. C. W. Stone, valued at $80" (*Kalamazoo Gazette* 1883). This artist is none other than Lucinda Stone's daughter-in-law Caroline Moore Stone (married to Clement Walker Stone) who traveled to Europe with Lucinda and studied art while there.

Caroline Moore Stone also contributed another painting titled *Portrait of Vittoria Colonna* to the LLA collection. In her "Saturday Talks" newspaper column, Lucinda Stone writes: "There is also upon the walls…a fine copy of the Victoria Colonna portrait of the Colonna Palace, Rome, the best authenticated portrait of this remarkable woman extant. This is by another lady formerly of Kalamazoo, Mrs. C. M. Stone" (L. H. Stone, "Saturday Talks" 1882). Indeed, a year earlier, the LLA treasurer's report of January 19, 1881, lists among disbursements $50 for the painting of Vittoria Colonna to Mrs. C. M. Stone (*Kalamazoo Daily Telegraph* 1881).

Who was this "remarkable" woman Vittoria Colonna? Perhaps the ladies knew of her from Longfellow's poem (1878) of the same name. Perhaps some had learned of her in art history courses as they studied Michelangelo. Vittoria Colonna (1492-1547) was an Italian noblewoman and poet. Upon the death of her husband, she retired to her castle and dedicated herself to writing poetry, mainly the Petrarchan sonnet (Vittoria Colonna 2010). When she was in her forties, she developed an artistic friendship with Michelangelo and they exchanged many letters and philosophical sonnets. Some have called Colonna "the female genius of the Italian Renaissance" (Vittoria Colonna n.d.). Girolao Muziano, who lived from 1532 to 1592, painted the original portrait.

✶ Above: A copy of *King Charles I and Queen Henrietta* by Anthony Van Dyke.
Page 107: A copy of *La Fornarina* by Sebastiano Del Piombo.

Another painting is *King Charles I and Queen Henrietta* by Anthony Van Dyke (1599-1641). This "double portrait," typical of the times, is a copy of one of the many portraits Van Dyke produced for the English nobility. The Flemish van Dyke established a brilliant career as court painter of Charles I of England. Queen Henrietta was born into a Catholic family in France. Her husband called her "Maria" and the Protestant English people (who never fully accepted her) called her "Queen Mary." She displayed courage and determination in mustering support for her husband and she was a lifelong supporter of the arts. She had nine children and lived 20 years after her husband who was beheaded in the English Civil Wars in 1649. Henrietta Maria is an ancestor of most of today's royal families (Henrietta Maria 2010).

The portrait titled *La Fornarina* hangs in the main library room. This is a copy of Sebastiano Del Piombo's original completed in 1512 (Amanti Art n.d.). The exact acquisition of this copy is undocumented. Mrs. Mason's anniversary poem of 1877 (mentioned in an earlier chapter) highlights the work: "Here's the gay Fornarina, whom Raphael loved / What wonder such charms the young painter's heart moved?" (Potts and Lyons-Jenness 1997, 24).

Most important to the collection is the large oil painting of Lucinda Hinsdale Stone. Lucinda's personal friend Mary B. Westnedge completed and signed this painting in 1897, three years before Lucinda's death. Mary Westnedge was the mother of Col. Joseph B. Westnedge, a member of a prominent longtime Kalamazoo family, who died in WWI. The family donated the portrait to the LLA some time after 1900. This portrait is not the first of Lucinda to hang in the LLA. An earlier portrait of a younger Lucinda, also done by Caroline Moore Stone, was given to the State Pioneer and Historical Society for display in the State Capitol Building in Lansing (L. H. Stone n.d.).

Lucinda Hinsdale Stone by Mary B. Westnedge

While many of the paintings are copies of the revered European masters, there is an original oil painting by the artist Laurits Holst called *Safe Harbor* (1870). This is a fine example of the Luminist school of American paintings. Although European-trained, Holst settled in Chicago and made a solid reputation with his popular and well-executed landscapes (Sheridan 2002). A committee of determined and frugal members traveled to Chicago to purchase this painting and others. The LLA minutes reported the following:

> "…Wishing to have a marine by Holst (a young Danish artist of great promise) the committee visited his studio, but found nothing within their means. After a good deal of discussion, in consideration of the picture being wanted for a public institution under the charge of *ladies,* he agreed to paint a view of the Golden Gate of his $500 size, for $200, and when it was completed, placed it in a $50 frame, which he presented to the Association" (LLA Board of Directors Meeting Minutes 1872).

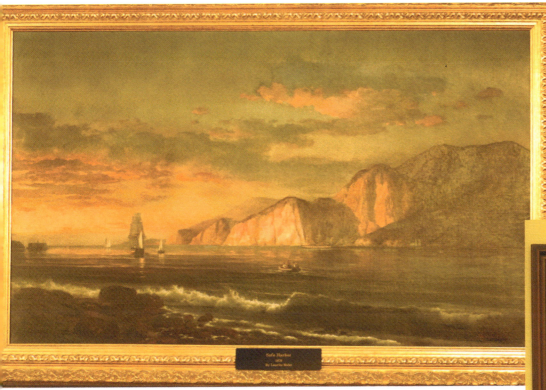

The allure and architecture of the Ladies' Library building have made it a favorite subject for local artists, particularly in the 20th century. The collection includes three renditions of the building. A charming pencil and watercolor drawing by Richard Gregg, completed in 1945, shows the building as it appeared over half a century ago. Gregg, a young man whose family lived nearby, studied art and eventually became a museum director. In 1971, Mrs. Donald S. Gilmore presented a framed etching to the LLA done by Alfred P. Maurice, former Gilmore Art Center director, who completed it while living in Kalamazoo. It shows the top section of the LLA building *(Kalamazoo Gazette* 1971). A third is a watercolor done in 1999 by Robin Leva Scheer, showing the building much as it appears today (Sheridan 2002).

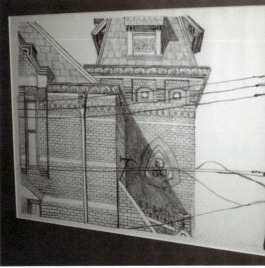

✸ Top clockwise: *Safe Harbor* by Laurits Holst; a pencil and watercolor drawing of the LLA building by Richard Gregg; etching of the LLA tower by Alfred P. Maurice; and watercolor of the LLA exterior by Robin Leva Scheer.

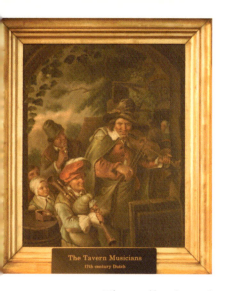  

The collection also includes the following copies: *The Tavern Musicians* possibly by Jan Steen; *The Journey,* a 17th century Italian genre painting; *The Melon Eaters* by Diego Velazquez; *The Council* by George Healy (1869); and two large photogravures, *Le Matin* by Bernier and *La Roche aux Mouettes* by Courant (1879). In the lending library room hangs a handsome painting titled *Portrait of a Man* thought to be a musician, possibly the young Beethoven. Smaller reproductions in the room include two copper plates, which depict *The Blue Boy* and *Master Lambton*. Such reproductions were popular souvenirs for many who traveled abroad, reminding the buyer of the original oils that still hang today in London's National Gallery.

In addition, there are six smaller paintings, all possibly of details of larger fresco paintings. The two lively *Cupids in Chariots* are on backgrounds of gold leaf in distinctive *Sgraffitto* frames. Two small circular paintings of angels (see page 99) are "gold ground," taken from the late medieval work of Fra Angelico (1395-1455) (Sheridan 2002).

❋ Top clockwise: Copies of *The Tavern Musicians, The Journey, The Melon Eaters* by Diego Velazquez, and *The Council* by George Healy; two photogravures titled *Le Matin* by Bernier and *LaRoche aux Mouettes* by Courant; *Portrait of a Man;* two gold leaf *Cupids in Chariots;* and two copper plate reproductions of *Master Lambton* and *The Blue Boy.*

110

Near the top of the front stairway hangs a print that represents all women who have participated in the club movement that culminated in the first half of the 20th century. David Robinson's *The Woman's Club* was originally published in *McCall's Magazine* in 1927, to illustrate the article "3,000,000 Women!" The original is in the General Federation of Women's Clubs headquarters in Washington, D.C. (LLA Newsletter 2014). Next to this painting is the drawing *Bronson Park* done in 1980 by Tim Callahan. It is clear from the full-grown trees in the park that the picture dates prior to May 13, 1980, when a tornado destroyed so many of the trees.

Finally, a studio portrait of another woman important to the LLA completes the art collection. Taken by well-known Kalamazoo photographer Lance Ferraro, the photo is of Virginia Earl, long-time professor of French and Spanish at Kalamazoo College. Earl, who died in 1999, endowed the LLA with a generous gift that enables the organization to continue its mission of literacy and children's education. More about Virginia Earl in Chapter 14.

❋ Top: A copy of *The Women's Club* by David Robinson; bottom: *Bronson Park* by Tim Callahan.

✶ A petit point picture of *Two Godey Ladies in a Garden* by Loretta Dingeman Vigneau.

Needlework

Historically, the needlework of women has rightfully been considered art. The first members initially brought their "fancy work" or knitting, to the monthly presentations. The LLA appropriately honors that tradition by including needlework in its art collection.

In the second floor reception area there is a petit point picture of two Godey Ladies in a garden. The work is a gift from Anna Baird, the granddaughter of Loretta Dingeman Vigneau (1886-1962) who created the work in three years during the early 1930s. The picture was framed at the J. L. Hudson Company of Detroit, Michigan.

In Philadelphia in 1830, Louis Antoine Godey began publishing the *Godey's Lady's Book,* which he designed to attract the growing audience of American women. The magazine was intended to entertain, inform, and educate the women of America. Early issues included biographical sketches, handcrafts, female costume, the dance, equestrienne procedures, health and hygiene, and recipes. In addition, the publishing of extensive fashion descriptions and plates became a vast reservoir of handsome hand-colored illustrations. These fashion plates appeared at the beginning of each issue and became a record of the progression in fashion during the years of publication, 1830-1898.

The illustrations were popularly repeated in needlework items and framed pictures. In 1836, Godey purchased the Boston-based *American Ladies' Magazine* and merged it with his. Sarah Josepha Hale (who incidentally wrote the nursery rhyme "Mary Had a Little Lamb,") was named editor. Mrs. Hale brought substance to the magazine and wrote frequently about the notion of "women's sphere." The magazine became the arbiter of taste to wealthy Americans, both men and women. Together Godey and Hale produced a magazine, which today is considered to be among the most important resources of 19th century American life and culture (Accessible-Archives.com 2011).

✻ Silk log cabin quilt by
  Mrs. Henry Brees in 1878.

Quilts

The LLA is fortunate to have three quilts that reflect its history and that of the Kalamazoo community. A small, silk log cabin quilt was made by Mrs. Henry Brees in 1878 as a part of a flurry of fundraising activities held to support the building fund. The quilt was raffled off for tickets purchased at fifty cents each, earning a total $106.50 (Potts and Lyons-Jenness 1997, 30). There is no record as to who won the raffle or how the quilt ended up back in the LLA building. Because of its fragility, the quilt is only displayed occasionally.

For many years, a large quilt made by members of the Kalamazoo Chapter of the Embroiderers Guild of America was displayed in the LLA auditorium. The quilt was designed and made in recognition of the City of Kalamazoo's Sesquicentennial in 1980. Taking over two years to complete, the quilt consists of 150 squares, which recall the first 150 years of Kalamazoo history. The first 40 squares give a chronological rendering of Kalamazoo's history from the Pottawatomi Indians to the 1980 tornado that wreaked havoc on downtown Kalamazoo and particularly Bronson Park. The next 110 squares give a topical view of industry, medical facilities, commerce and transportation, the arts, education and miscellaneous (Kalamazoo Chapter of The Embroiderers Guild of America 1980). This quilt now hangs in the upstairs hallway outside the auditorium door. Besides marveling at the beauty of the quilt, visitors enjoy reminiscing about places and events from the past.

The third quilt also on display is above the elevator door in the back hallway of the first floor. The LLA members made this piece in 2002 for the 150th anniversary of their organization. The quilt depicts representations significant to the LLA including a yellow rose, a bus for the yearly trips to Chicago, a Christmas tree for the annual holiday decorating of the building, and the Books for Babies project among others.

Both the Embroiderers Guild quilt and the LLA anniversary quilt were hung in the LLA auditorium until the 21st Century Project of 2013. It was during that time when experts informed the members that the quilts (along with the carpeting) absorbed sound and affected the acoustics of the space. The quilts and carpeting were removed and the quilts were relocated elsewhere in the building.

✳ Quilt honoring LLA's 150th Anniversary in 2002.

✳ Quilt sewn by Kalamazoo Chapter of the Embroiders Guild of America honoring Kalamazoo's Sesquicentennial Anniversary in 1980.

✱ Legend for the sesquicentennial quilt.

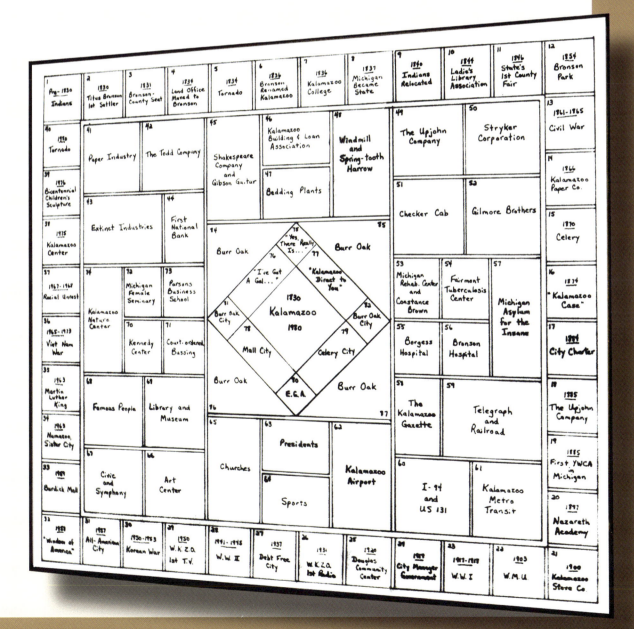

Chapter 12 *Furniture*

"In the old pieces of furniture as in the old paintings, dwells the charm of the past..."
—- Adalbert Swifter (from the book *Indian Summer*)

Like the building itself, many of the furnishings are distinctive. When the new building was opened, the furnishings were valued at $6,000. While the provenance of every piece of furniture has not been documented, it is believed that Ruth Webster donated the "president's chair" and a sofa.

❋ Page 118: President's chair donated by Ruth Webster.
❋ Page 119: Sofa also donated by Ruth Webster.

❋ Top: Ornate library desk; middle left: Detail of desk leg; middle center: Detail of turned wooden desk brace; middle right: Intricately carved desk lock plate; bottom: Striped sofa in main library room.

Those Webster pieces and several other existing pieces can be identified in vintage photographs. The long striped sofa presently in the main library room is shown in an early picture with a tufted back. These tufts must have been lost in a subsequent reupholstering. Both the ornate library desk and the small, simple wooden chair used with it can be identified in one of the earliest photos. The House Committee report of 1997 states "a dismantled old chair found in the basement has been rehabilitated and is now being used with the desk on the main floor." How fortunate that the broken chair pieces were not thrown away (LLA House Committee Report 1997)!

Eight of the original small, velvet-upholstered folding chairs have been retained in honor of the eight original members: Miss Susan Rice, Mrs. Lyman Kendall, Mrs. D. B. Webster, Mrs. A. S. Kedzie, Mrs. William Dennison, Mrs. Alexis Ransom, Mrs. K. May Gibbs, and Mrs. Lucinda Hinsdale Stone. Engraved brass nameplates were added to the chairs in 2004.

❋ Top left: Restored chair used with library desk; top right: Velvet upholstered folding chairs in honor of the eight original LLA members; lower right: New red upholstered auditorium chairs with walnut metal woodgrain frames.

In 1905, Mrs. J. W. Walker of Chicago (formerly Ella Marsh of Kalamazoo) offered a Steinway grand piano to the LLA. The piano was later purchased from Mrs. Walker by the LLA for $850, and today is valued at more than $15,000. It was restored, rebuilt, and refinished during the restoration project of 1974-1979. Ruth Van Haaften donated a second piano for the main library room in 1985. This one was eventually replaced by a new piano in 2012 in memory of past president Virginia Norton.

✺ Page 122 top: Steinway grand piano located on the auditorium stage; bottom left: Steinway logo; bottom middle: Carved lyre and foot pedals; bottom right: Cast metal plate denotes the manufacturer's date of June 13, 1870.

✺ Page 123: Upright piano in main library room donated in memory of Virginia Norton.

❋ Antique settee located in the second floor foyer.

Members and friends continued to donate items in the 1980s and 1990s. Beth Kinch donated an "antique settee" and Mrs. Charles Mangee gave her antique library table, a perfect complement to the interior. In 2012, Shirley Shane donated two small church pews for the auditorium. A cellaret in the main library room commemorates the efforts of Tamara Roberts who worked in the kitchen. The brass plate on the front reads: "She served with love and grace."

❋ Top left: Fine wood table located in the lending library alcove; top right: Church pew; bottom: Cellaret.

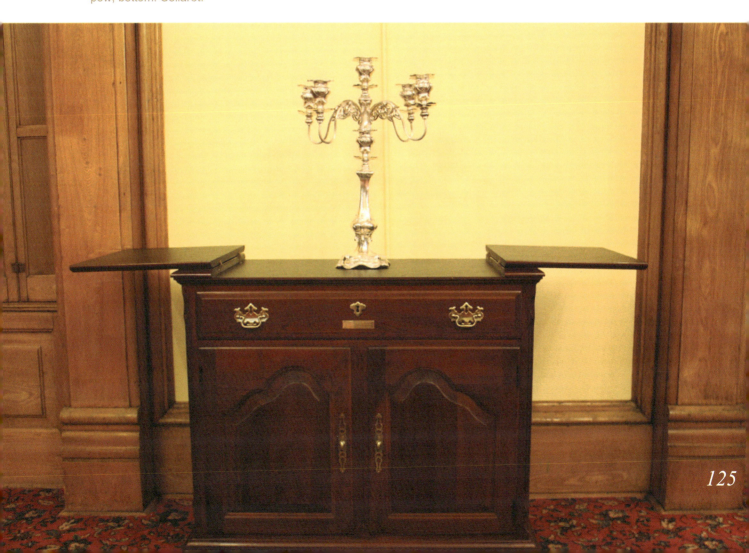

The Lawton Sofa

In 2013, Kalamazoo resident Valerie Opdyke donated a Victorian sofa to the LLA that originally belonged to her great-grandparents. They transported it from Seneca Falls, New York, to Kalamazoo around 1865. Opdyke's grandparents, Charles DeWitt Lawton and his wife Lucy Lovina Latham Lawton bought land in Van Buren County in 1865 and built their home in the village that became known as Lawton, Michigan. The Empire-style sofa's original upholstery would have been horsehair. Opdyke's donation included information about the family, a brief history of the couch, and even a vintage photo of Mr. Lawton reclining on the sofa reading a book.

Mr. Lawton was Chair of Engineering at the University of Michigan in 1870, and he and his brother brought the first grape plantings to Van Buren County from New York in 1865-66. Mrs. Lawton established the Isabella Club in Lawton and traveled with Lucinda Stone in 1893 to the Columbian Exposition in Chicago.

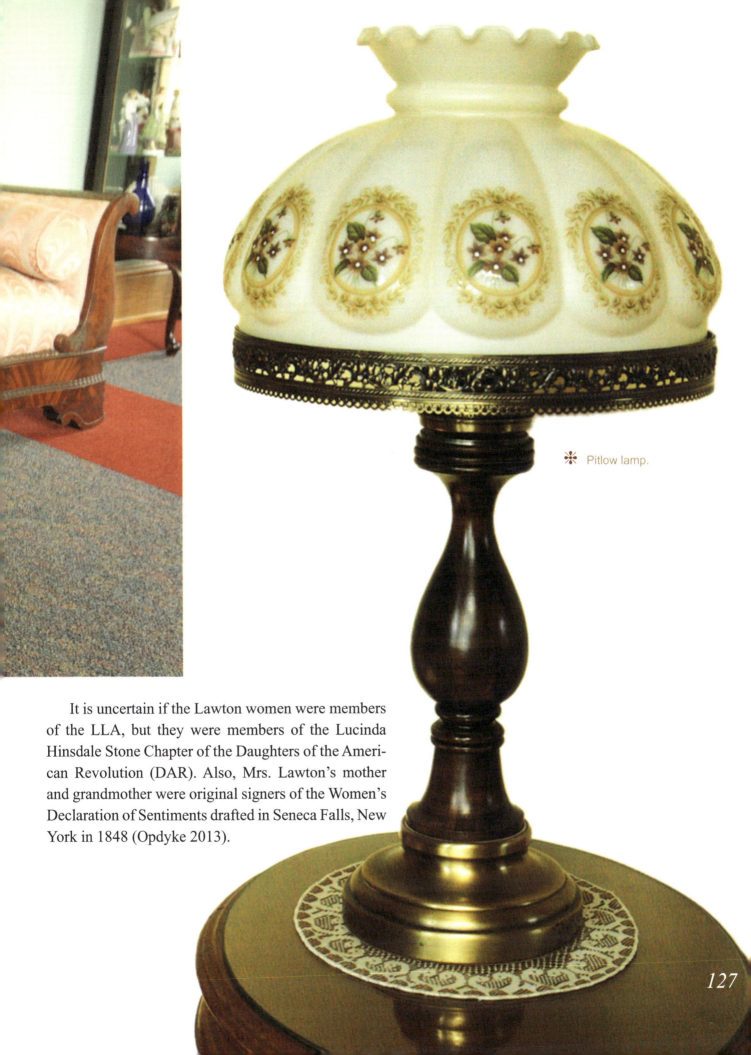

Pitlow lamp.

It is uncertain if the Lawton women were members of the LLA, but they were members of the Lucinda Hinsdale Stone Chapter of the Daughters of the American Revolution (DAR). Also, Mrs. Lawton's mother and grandmother were original signers of the Women's Declaration of Sentiments drafted in Seneca Falls, New York in 1848 (Opdyke 2013).

Chapter 13
Becoming Barrier-Free

"...invariably when we design something that can be used by those with disabilities, we often make it better for everyone."
-- Donald Norman
(American scientist)

❋ Top: Directional sign leading to accessible entrance; bottom: Accessible automatic door opener post.

❋ Page 131: South walk leading to the accessible entrance and memorial garden.

The passage of the Americans with Disabilities Act (ADA) approved by Congress in 1990 and associated publicity of this legislation, created an awareness of the lack of accessibility for persons with limited mobility in many older public and semi-public buildings. The ADA affected all new and existing buildings—both public and privately owned, when used as public accommodations.

The ADA regulations excluded private clubs and religious facilities when activities in the facilities were for members. However, when these buildings were used for events involving persons other than members, i.e., the general public, they became public accommodations. Therefore, many churches and private club buildings, like the LLA, began making changes to comply with the ADA accessibility guidelines to extend their use beyond activities for those who were not members.

It was evident that some members of the LLA were no longer able to climb stairs to attend club activities. It was also noted some organizations that used the LLA for various functions had persons in their groups who could not climb steps or use their wheelchairs to enter the building. In some instances, these organization's participants carried those individuals in and out of the building with risk to both the assisted and the carrier.

Various ideas were pursued. One of these ideas provided a ramp, allowing access up the front steps to the building entry. Unfortunately, such a ramp would be far too long for the space allowed to place it and still would only give access to the first floor. Steps were still necessary to reach either of the undersized water closets.

The next idea was a small lift that would be located at the southwest corner of the building to move people between the first and second floors. Dorothy and Herman Dykema had this idea and

worked on it for some time. It would require one small water closet to be made into a unisex bathroom that would be located only on the second floor. This idea also involved acquiring some property from the Kalamazoo Civic Theatre parking lot for the entryway to the elevator. Some costs projections were compiled, but no action was taken.

As years passed, new fire and safety regulations were added to the building and trade codes. Not only was the building accessibility a problem, but new regulations regarding fire exits were now in effect. Besides the wide main staircase in the front foyer, the LLA building had a single stairway from the second floor that opened into the kitchen. This was no longer allowed as a safe fire exit. In 2008, the subject of an elevator was often suggested, but it was felt that the rules for historical integrity would prevent this installation.

Richard Baker, a retired and registered architect (and husband of active member Barbara Baker) was familiar with the building. He designed some plans to expand the building to the east into the memorial garden. His plans included an elevator that gave access into the building and to the second floor, accessible bathrooms for the disabled, and a fire exit that would be in compliance with the current building and fire codes. He shared this plan with the LLA, but no action was taken at that time.

The building limitations and liabilities became obvious, but the task of correction was somewhat overwhelming. Mr. Baker contacted Nelson Nave, a historic renovation architect, and asked him to prepare a proposal for necessary architectural services. Nave was asked to complete the design and details for approval by historical building interests, and estimate a preliminary cost for the work. Nelson was a member of the City of Kalamazoo Historic Commission and was very familiar with the approval processes required for modifying federal and state registered historic buildings. Initially Richard referred to this project as the 21st Century Update.

In 2009-2010, the elevator idea was pursued, but again no formal action was taken. In June 2011, LLA President Mary Bower arranged a meeting with Richard Baker, Lois Richmond (First Vice President), and Shirley Shane who had worked on the problem earlier. During her career at Bronson Hospital in Nursing Administration, Richmond also worked as the nursing consultant for major construction projects at the hospital. She had worked with various architects, builders, etc., and saw the plan as very doable and necessary.

Richard informed the small group of Nave's prior interest in providing architectural service for the project. It was agreed to continue pursuing the plan and take it to the LLA Board of Directors for

approval. December of 2011, the Board of Directors voted to move forward with the plans for an elevator and ADA-compliant bathrooms. Initial funds were approved by the Board to develop cost estimates for further study. A summary of the results of the now officially named "21st Century Project" is in Chapter 14.

✻ Top left: Accessible double-door entrance; top right: Elevator; bottom: Ground level foyer.

Chapter 14
21st Century

"Without continual growth and progress, such words as improvement, achievement, and success have no meaning."
-- Benjamin Franklin (American founding father, statesman, inventor, author)

Virginia Earl

Virginia Elizabeth Earl was born on August 6, 1904, in Kalamazoo and lived there the majority of her life. She was the only daughter of Otis and Lora Earl. Her father was president of the Kalamazoo Board of Education beginning in 1920 (Michigan Pioneer and Historical Society n.d.) and was a prominent patent attorney in western Michigan (Kalamazoo Public Library n.d.). Virginia worked in her father's law office on occasion and never married.

She graduated from Kalamazoo Central High School and continued her studies at Kalamazoo College where she graduated in 1926 (Kalamazoo College Alumnus 1957). She furthered her education at the University of Michigan, earning both education and arts degrees. For two years she taught high school English and French in St. Johns, Michigan. Later she taught French and Spanish at Kalamazoo College until her retirement.

She was active in the University of Michigan Women's Club and the American Association of University Women. Ms. Earl was never an LLA member, but she often attended meetings as a guest of her mother who joined in 1921 (LLA Membership Lists 1914-1941). Because she was not a member, Virginia's generous legacy to the organization was a surprise.

Upon her death on October 25, 1999 (*Kalamazoo Gazette* 1999), she bequeathed her estate equally to four organizations—the Kalamazoo Public Library / Kalamazoo Valley Museum, the Salvation Army, the Shriners Hospital for Children in Chicago, and, yes, to the Ladies' Library Association of Kalamazoo. After legal issues were resolved regarding intent of the will, more than two million dollars was reflected in the Treasurer's report of the LLA Board of Directors meeting minutes on May 1, 2003.

This gift established a much-needed safety net for the building's future. The back garden renovation was made possible by a small portion of this bequest and was dedicated to Virginia Earl's memory. Her photograph hangs in a place of honor next to the Ruth Webster Memorial Window.

❋ Page 137: Virginia Earl portrait, located in the main library room, photo originally taken by Lance Ferraro.

137

21st Century Project Summary

The original library building was constructed in 1878, long before standardized construction codes and ordinances were established for any building. At that time, the greatest threat was fire—not only for the loss of life, but the loss of a building itself. Building codes (as we now know them) came along at the turn of the century (1900s). Ironically, the first "building codes" were focused heavily on sanitation rather than the building structure. An examination of the original construction drawings for the Ladies' Library building reveals they primarily addressed the artistic details and materials used in the building, and secondarily, some guidance for how the building would be heated.

Electric street lighting went into effect in downtown Kalamazoo in 1886. At some point between 1886 and the late 1920s (just prior to the first addition to the building) electricity was added and some plumbing, essential for serving food and coffee. The preparation and serving of food for a fundraiser was part of the organization's activity, so this modification would have been required. There was obviously a need for at least one toilet in the building. At the annual meeting in 1890, a report was given that a cloakroom and new lavatory were built for $287 and the first toilet paper was purchased for 25 cents. The small room at the north end of the lending library room is presumed to be its location, as examination of the subfloor under the north wall of this small room shows floor openings for water supply and drainage piping.

The first major renovation to the building took place in 1931 with the addition of a kitchen, two small bathrooms, two dressing rooms, and a stor-

✱ 1974-1979 building restoration commemoration plaque; middle: One of four accessible restrooms.

age room. (More about this in Chapters 6 and 8.) The second renovation and restoration project took place in 1978.

In 1974, an architect was hired to evaluate needed repairs. Members were astounded at the $140,000 estimate. The decision was made to proceed with the project and a four-year fund drive began to accumulate the necessary capital. Past board minutes and other archival material regarding the Association record numerous occasions of fundraising, grants, loans, and miscellaneous gathering of funds to repair and maintain the historic structure. Leaks in the roof haunted the organization! The women who came before did their best to seek the most capable craftsmen to work on the building and keep it in good shape. The rehabilitation project in 1978 involved work on the interior and the exterior. Notes say "too many repairs to list." Some of the interior work included having the paintings and chandeliers cleaned and some of the furniture reupholstered.

In 2008, the organization struggled with the accessibility problem. Concerns continued as to how to improve the building. In 2011, safety issues became paramount. The lack of an approved fire escape, inadequate accessibility to the building for the disabled (or those who just had difficulty in climbing stairs), and code violations led many members to think more about corrective action.

Some members, however, felt nothing could be done because of the restrictions of the historic commission and were fearful of the high cost of the proposed changes. The need for the organization to move forward was favored and at the Board of Directors meeting in December of 2011, the Board approved the motion to review the cost and a plan of action. Money was allocated to hire an architect to draw initial plans and provide estimates of costs. This plan would be called the 21st Century Project.

Architect Richard Baker (who had worked on previous plans) suggested Nelson Nave be consulted to do the preliminary blueprints and estimates. Nave specialized in historic restoration. The LLA was fortunate that those who came before had purchased a vacant lot behind the building, giving room for the addition. The addition would provide a full-size elevator, four accessible bathrooms, and a reception area on the first and second floors. These updates would also make the building ADA-compliant, correct the electrical and plumbing code violations, and provide an approved fire escape. In addition, a licensed kitchen would finally become a reality and rehabilitation of all clear glass windows would be complete.

Nehil and Sivak (structural engineers) were contracted to evaluate the structural integrity of the building. Miller-Davis Construction

139

Company was contracted to do the project since they had completed the only other addition to the building in 1931. A geological survey with soil borings and an asbestos survey were performed.

A construction committee of LLA members was selected and began meeting weekly in preparation for the construction phase. LLA members Barbara Baker, Topsy Schlegel, Judy Sherrod, Lisa Salay, and chair Lois Richmond were joined on the committee by Miller-Davis representatives Karen Gruss (project manager), Jim Buckhout (construction manager), and Nelson Nave. Together they worked as an on-call team through weekends and holidays until the project was complete.

A general housecleaning of documents and scrapbooks was arranged by Barbara Baker and done by members of the Ways & Means Committee. Sharon Carlson, Director of Archives and Regional History at the Charles C. and Lynn L. Zhang Legacy Collections Center at Western Michigan University, supervised the activity by helping to determine what should be saved and what could be discarded. Most of the saved documents were then sent to the WMU archives.

House Chair, Shirley Shane worked with Mulders Moving and Storage and volunteers to pack up art pieces and sculptures to store on site during the construction. When construction was completed everything was unpacked and put back in place. An inventory of kitchen items also was done at this time.

Plans to have a community fundraising campaign were held and the Owen Group was selected to coordinate this aspect of the project. The Earl endowment fund gave the financial base on which to secure a bank loan. Some very helpful grants from the Gilmore Foundation, the Harold and Grace Upjohn Foundation, and the W. S. and Lois Van Dalson Foundation were applied for and

✻ Top: 21st Century Project ground-breaking ceremony, holding shovels (left to right) are Christine Ballard, Betty Weston, Nancy Norton, and Lois Richmond.

received. Adequate funds were procured to do the project.

Over the years, boundaries had been compromised for various reasons and needed to be definitively determined. Gregory Jensen was requested to conduct a new property survey and property lines were negotiated with neighbors. On the north, a previous 1904 alley agreement made with the resident at that time, clarified the use of the shared driveway space. The area to the east and north was shared with the First Presbyterian Church for many years. Now the property line on the north had to be shared for the benefit of both parties. A new fence was installed, giving the LLA the space required to place windows on the north side of the new addition and giving the church adequate space to build an equipment structure.

The east property line had been compromised with three feet of space temporarily used by the First Presbyterian Church as a walkway. This property was reclaimed by the LLA. Negotiations allowed contractors to tunnel electrical connections to security cameras on LLA property for the church. Also, the LLA's sewer line was tied to that of the church for possible overflow into the city sewer line, if necessary.

The south property line bordering the Kalamazoo Civic Theatre parking lot was divided with heavy guardrails to prevent cars from driving into the building. Records in the archives stipulated these guardrails were installed by the LLA to protect the building. A new fence was placed on the LLA property line and the heavy guardrail was removed. Establishing this property line gave evidence that the building was built askew on the property.

The Memorial Garden was re-planted, keeping as much of the original details as possible. Original pavers were mixed with new pavers to

✻ Top: 21st Century Campaign recognition board.

✻ Top: Foyer view of door to powder room and kitchen sealed during the 21st Century Project; middle: Door between renovated kitchen and new Area of Refuge; bottom: Automatic external defibrillator mounted on the wall in the main library room.

✻ Page 143 top: Renovated kitchen; bottom left: New cooking ranges, ovens, and air handling system; bottom right: Sign designating Area of Refuge.

complete the area. New outdoor lights were installed and the old ones were sold.

The kitchen renovation included the elimination of a small powder room, the back door, and the stairway from the second floor. Cabinetry was moved within the kitchen and a new storage pantry and secure silver storage cabinet were added. Two new cooking ranges replaced the outdated model and an extensive air handling system assures proper ventilation. Two new freezers were donated, one placed in the kitchen storage area of the basement. The back exit from both floors now allows entrance into an Area of Refuge, a location to hold occupants during a fire or other emergency, until they can be rescued.

In the past, the auditorium was used for lectures, meetings, and music events enjoyed by many in the community. But in recent years it was seldom used outside of club events. Carpet, wall hangings, and stage drapes were removed to improve acoustics. A beautiful original Michigan white pine floor was discovered under the horsehair pad and thick carpet.

One transom window (the Bryant) fell from its fasteners during construction. Jamie Rife, who had previously designed and built the *Lines of Knowledge* window, worked many hours to repair and re-install it. Old Home Rehabilitation Company did the major rehabilitation of the other windows.

Individual stones were tapped out of the original basement wall to make the initial opening into the new portion of the basement. Steel reinforcement of the existing basement was necessary to prevent shifting of the building. An old coal bin was discovered in this area from the original heating system. This new opening into the original building was coined "Nave's Cave" in honor of the architect.

A new sump pump was installed in the basement floor to provide a necessary drainage in the event of a major leak from the hot water heaters.

The basement was divided into individual rooms, and walls and fire doors were installed for improved fire protection.

The 21st Century Project was very beneficial to the building and allows complete use of all of the building for years to come. Along with the completion of the project, new safety procedures were implemented since use of the building was increasing. Two mock fire drills were held to review instructions for evacuating the building. An Automatic Emergency Defibrillator (AED) was purchased and other life-saving procedures were reviewed. A roof access unit was installed in the new stairway to provide periodic inspection and repairs, as necessary, and a preventative maintenance program will continue to maintain this beautiful historic landmark.

The 21st Century Project added 950 square feet on each of the three floors, for a total of 2,850 square feet. That, added to the existing 7,484 square-foot building, makes a grand total 10,334 square feet of usable space. The total renovation cost was approximately $1.7 million. In the fall of 2014, the debt to complete the initial project was paid in full. A licensed kitchen, ADA compliance, and a new parking lot now offer renewed opportunities to share the building with the community.

On September 25, 2015, the LLA was presented with the Historical Society of Michigan's Restoration / Preservation Award for the restoration of the building. Sharon Carlson nominated the LLA for the award and presented it to Past President Lois Richmond and President Paula Jamison. The honor was celebrated at the 141st Annual State History Conference at Saginaw Valley State University.

Challenges Facing the 21st Century

Installing an elevator at 333 South Park Street and making the historic building ADA compliant was not without its challenges. The issue had been discussed and researched twice in five years.

Once the Board approved the project, there was much concern among the LLA membership about such an ambitious, costly endeavor. The project evolved into something much larger than just adding an elevator. Healthy debate is good, and the 21st Century Project and LLA membership were not to be left out of this discourse. Committee chair Lois Richmond, held multiple meetings to give every member the opportunity to ask questions and state their concerns. The meetings were scheduled over a period of several months. Lois even made personal visits to member homes to gather input on the project.

The real work began after Richmond selected the 21st Century Committee. The team moved through the process of hiring an architect, a general contractor, and subcontractors. Setbacks were expected and were dealt with throughout the project. Some problems were small and others more complicated. Patience, determination, and most importantly, humor were necessary in order to be a part of this committee. The future holds the story for the next chapter of the building. History will determine its legacy.

The 341 Property Acquisition

Throughout LLA's existence downtown lots have been at a premium. Early on, the organization shared the surrounding properties with residences. Gradually these residences were torn down and replaced with commercial buildings and parking lots. Soon the LLA clubhouse was landlocked and parking became a real issue. A neighbor across the street, the Kalamazoo Institute of Arts (KIA), graciously allowed LLA members to use their parking lots on Mondays when the KIA was closed. However, parking on other days was not available there. On-street parking was also available (using meters at peak times).

With the completion of the 21st Century Project more events were held. The parking situation became critical. Across the street to the south of the LLA property (on the corner of Lovell and Park Streets) stood a building that once housed an answering service company. It was built in 1963 as an annex to the People's Church that was razed in 1968. The lot consisted of a building and a good-sized parking lot. The property had been for sale for years, but with the 21st Century Project requiring much of the LLA's resources, it was not advisable to purchase at that time. However, in October of 2013, LLA President Lois Richmond and her husband James seized the opportunity and gave designated funds to purchase the property for the LLA.

Discussions then began regarding how to use the building. The biggest challenge was that the building was not barrier-free. Suggestions included razing the building, using it as an annex to the LLA building, renting it to another non-profit organization, or selling just the building. In the end, the only sensible solution was to raze the building and to reconstruct the entire property into parking space. As of the fall of 2015, the LLA has a beautiful parking lot with 29 parking spaces and two barrier-free spaces. The LLA now has parking for members and guests.

✸ New LLA parking lot.

Chapter 15 *Basement*

"It is in the shelter of each other that people live."
-- Irish proverb

❋ Original stone, brick, and mortar coal bin removed during the renovation.

The walls of the basement are stone and mortar, quite typical of the way Michigan basements were constructed. There were no permanent partitions in the original basement. Pegboard divided areas holding Christmas and other event decorations, items for the holiday bazaar and patio sale, unused furniture, and other storage needs. The renovation project in 2013 led to the installation of walls and fire-rated doors on each of the ten rooms. Three furnaces and three air conditioners provide heat and cool air for the total building.

Renovations helped create an office in the basement, two elevator maintenance rooms, a housekeeping room, furnace, custodian, chair storage rooms, kitchen storage, two general storage rooms, and an open work area.

There is an interesting original arch doorway at the west entrance of the basement at the bottom of the stairs. Water faucets and a drain in the new housekeeping room were provided in the basement addition. Now the original basement ceilings (more than eight-feet high) have windows at street level on three sides and bright new electric lighting.

❋ Page 149: Photo collage of basement improvements.

149

Chapter 16
Garden

"A garden is not made by singing 'O How Beautiful,' and sitting in the shade."
-- Rudyard Kipling
(English author)

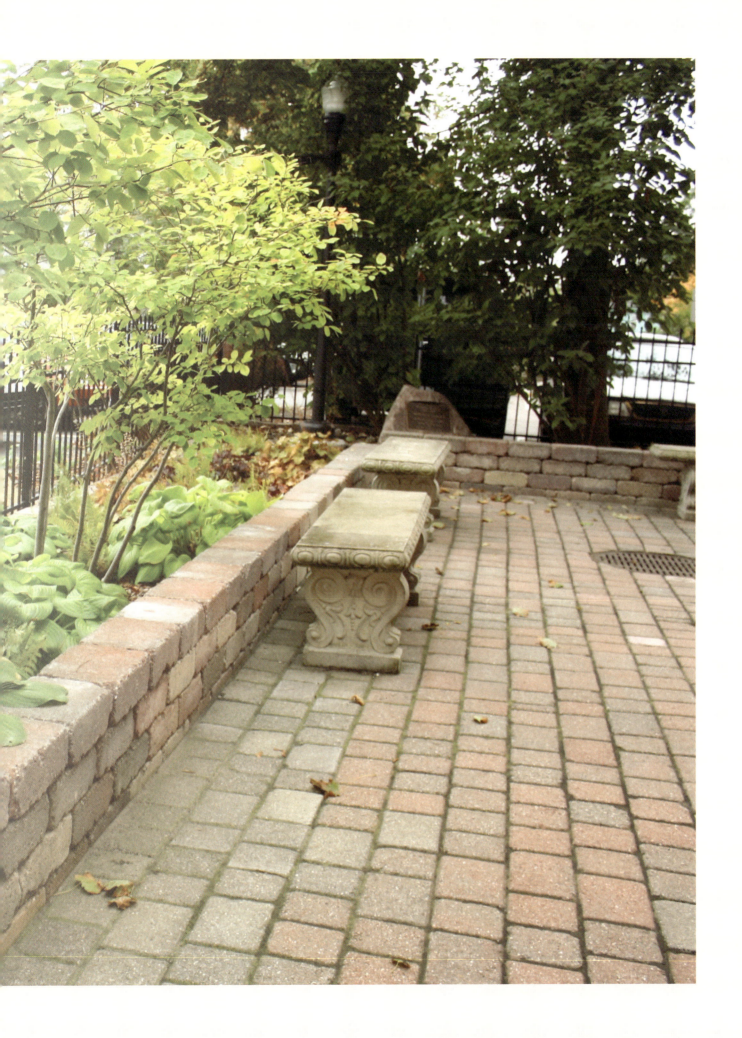

✳ Page 152: Virginia Earl Memorial Garden plaque.

P rior to the creation of the Virginia Earl Memorial Garden in 2002, the perimeter of the "backyard" consisted mostly of scrub growth and iris along the north side of the building. There were also tulips and tree saplings on the east side. The south side of the property contained volunteer trees and scrub growth. Growing on the west side, against the building, were snowball bushes and various saplings. Shade trees and tree roots minimized growth of grass. This design was maintained for approximately 25 years.

Once the new design of the memorial garden was completed and approved, ground breaking commenced. The First Presbyterian Church was kind enough to permit the LLA use of their parking lot as a staging area for equipment and materials. Sod, shrubs, and trees were removed in 2002. The entire area was replaced with brick pavers and landscaped with fencing and curbing. The final touches were well-placed benches, sculptures, and lampposts, all at a cost of $26,000 (D. Dykema, Maintenance Verification Form for the State Historic Preservation Office 2006).

The Virginia Earl Memorial Garden was completed and dedicated on May 6, 2002. Dorothy Dykema used the Kipling quote (on this chapter opening) for the dedication, and the words still hold true today. Ladies' Library Association member Annmarie Freeland and her husband, Wesley, donated a boulder with a mounted plaque in honor of Virginia Earl. The boulder was prepared and set by the Patten Monument Company.

The statuary was chosen and purchased while the landscaping was being completed. However, according to Tim Eschelbach (the landscape architect from DeYoung Landscape), the installation took place after their work was completed. Although there is little known history of the statuary, it has been stated that members of the Garden Club carefully chose the pieces. One is of a young boy carrying books and the other is of a young girl reading a book. This suggests they were chosen to symbolize the strong dedication the LLA has toward children and literacy (D. Dykema, LLA Garden Dedication Address 2002).

✳ Left: Statue of boy carrying books; right: Statue of young girl reading.

During the 2006-2007 LLA calendar year, three trees (one Japanese Maple and two Serviceberry trees) were added to the Earl Garden to replace a large tree that had been removed. The Japanese maple was planted to honor the memory of long-time member Betty Wolbers. Donations were received from members of the LLA, the Portage Garden Club, and the Kalamazoo Network to help defray the cost of the project. A plaque was placed in front of the maple tree (LLA 2006-2007 House Committee Annual Report 2007).

Although the garden is hidden in the middle of Kalamazoo's Central Business District, it continues to be a place of solace and serenity for those who walk up the path and pass through its gate.

❋ Page 154: Perennial garden bed.

❋ Page 155 top left: Japanese Maple tree; top right: Betty Wolbers memorial plaque; middle: Garden bench leg detail; bottom left: Path from garden to Park Street; bottom right: Place of quiet solitude.

Chapter 17 *Special Celebrations*

"The more you praise and celebrate your life, the more there is in life to celebrate."
-- Oprah Winfrey
(TV personality and philanthropist)

❋ Page 159: LLA file photo collage of member activities and celebrations.

From their inception, the Ladies' Library Association membership focused on the intellectual improvement of the group with programs on art, literature, science, education, and history. Whenever a special building need arose, the Association raised funds by sponsoring social celebrations and events for members and the community. As early as 1859, the minutes of the LLA mention a strawberry and ice cream social. Early events were held in rented rooms decorated with evergreens and flowers. These gatherings often featured musical and poetic presentations. As money was collected, it was saved for the building fund or later used to repair the leaking roof.

Because of the organization's emphasis on literacy and educational programming, the original architectural drawings for the new building did not include space for food preparation or dining (Schmitt 1976, 332). After construction, the ladies served the first tea in their new building in 1890. Teas for members and guests were well attended and ice cream socials were a favorite among many.

A decorative arts exhibition was held for the community in 1889. Paintings, artwork done by members, and collections of small items were also on exhibit to create a welcoming atmosphere for these events. The directors and officers were often very generous with flowers and decorations from their own home gardens (Potts and Lyons-Jenness 1997, 65).

By 1926, the Finance Committee became responsible for food sales, bridge parties, luncheons, and Christmas card sales (Potts and Lyons-Jenness 1997, 73). From 1936 to 1940 members held rummage sales and sold Christmas fruitcakes. Items culled from LLA cupboards and bookcases were also sold to raise money to support the operations of the building (Potts and Lyons-Jenness 1997, 76-78). Many celebrations and events continued throughout the years.

In the late 1980s, a few functions became annual events: the June ice cream social, the holiday Lucinda's Attic Bazaar, the Past Presidents luncheon, and a marathon bridge party. Two annual luncheons helped to support the General Federation of Women's Club projects, namely Girlstown Foundation (now Guiding Harbor) and Operation Smile. Over time, events involving food service became popular with members and the community. The Ways & Means Committee continues to raise funds to pay for building maintenance and equipment upgrades.

Each milestone anniversary of the Association was commemorated with special events that included appropriate addresses, reminiscences, printed programs, inspirational readings, music, and refreshments. In her book *Women With a Vision*, Grace Potts described in detail the 25th anniversary celebration of 1877 and the golden anniversary of 1902. The program for the 1902 celebration consisted of remembrances of the past and Mrs. John den Bleyker wrote and read a history of the club (LLA Membership Lists 1914-1941). The year 1927 marked the 75th anniversary celebration. For this

event, Association historian Florence G. Mills wrote a 25-year summary of the LLA's activities, enumerating the programs and lectures given on such topics as travel, works of literature, homemaking, and literacy (LLA "Seventy-Five Years: L.L.A." Summary 1927).

The Association's centennial celebration was held in 1952. A banquet was held at Western Michigan College's union building with several invited guests from county, state, and national Federation groups (Potts and Lyons-Jenness 1997, 86). The event program noted that the Western Michigan College String Trio provided music, and officers of the General Federation of Women's Clubs gave the guest addresses (LLA Centennial Program 1952).

In 1979, the Association celebrated the 100th anniversary of the building with a "reenactment" of the original dedication ceremony. As part of the festivities Representative Mary C. Brown, State Senator Edgar Fredericks, and Representative Robert Welborn presented Senate and House resolutions commending the LLA for past and present endeavors in the community. Judge Robert B. Borsos served as "president of the evening" and introduced the program as well as paraphrased his predecessor's remarks:

> The first purpose of the LLA was to establish a library for the village of Kalamazoo and the ladies were told to gather books of concern to women—sewing, cooking, etc. "Stay away from controversy and avoid thoughts not fit for women," the 1879 judge said.
>
> Borsos' remarks on the present day role of women were tinged with humor, as he said, "A hundred years later we see there was a lot of wisdom in this advice" (Kalamazoo Gazette, 1979, p. 1979).

The Sesquicentennial Celebration of May 6, 2002, included two noteworthy achievements. First was the dedication of the Virginia Earl Memorial Garden. A plaque and statue in the garden signify the steadfastness to the ideals of the Ladies' Library and involvement with literacy and children (D. Dykema, LLA Garden Dedication Address 2002). Second was the announcement of the commission of the new stained-glass commemorative window, *Lines of Knowledge*, to be funded by the bequest of Fern and Herbert Rodewald.

    Commemorating 160 years of existence became a very special, week-long celebration. Under the direction of President Lois Richmond, the events of May 14-18, 2012, included a garden reception, the annual meeting luncheon, a brunch, and a high tea. Special guests for the week were three of Lucinda Hinsdale Stone's great-great-granddaughters—Elizabeth Harris, Katharine Brooker, and Alice Hurd. Elizabeth spoke at the luncheon, sharing research for her forthcoming biography on Lucinda and read from Lucinda's sketches.

    At the brunch, First Vice President Paula Jamison and her husband Frank Jamison presented highlights of their new video production *Dare to Know* about the Ladies' Library. The highlight of the high tea was the presentation of *Our Story—Dreams and Visions, 1852-2012,* an original chamber theatre production based on the life of Lucinda H. Stone. This was written and directed by June Cottrell, professor emerita of theater, Western Michigan University (LLA Celebration Week Program 2012).

On May 18, 2014, a community open house celebrated the completion of the 21st Century Project. This distinguished event included remarks from Association Past President Lois Richmond, special piano music by member Helen Lukan Brown, the premier of "When a Stone Sings" (cello solo composed for this event and performed by Elizabeth Start), and appropriate remarks by Michigan legislators Margaret O'Brien and Sean McCann (LLA Dedication Program 2014).

❋ Pages 160-161: LLA scrapbook photos of the 160th anniversary celebration.

Today, approximately 70 events are scheduled each year to help support building operations. Volunteers from the Ways & Means Committee, under the direction of Barbara Baker, continue to prepare food and offer program support. Another committee provides decorations for LLA events, special occasions, and holidays. A ceiling-high Victorian Christmas tree, wreaths and swags on bookcase tops, and colorful linens add to the festive atmosphere in the main library and the auditorium.

To brighten the room at other times of the year, tables may have scarecrows, angels, bookend vases, and flowers and greenery from members' gardens. These celebrations and the work and planning that are required to conduct them provide members with a variety of opportunities to serve the organization in creative, social, and entertaining ways.

❋ Page 162: Food prepared and presented by the Ways & Means Committee.

❋ Page 163: Seasonal and special event displays and dressings by the Decorations Committee.

Chapter 18
Heart and Soul of LLA

"Any time women come together with a collective intention, it's a powerful thing. Whether it's sitting down making a quilt, in a kitchen preparing a meal, in a club reading the same book, or around the same table playing cards, or planning a birthday party, when women come together with a collective intention, magic happens."

-- Phylicia Rashad
(American actress)

Ladies' Library

Three friends, a reading circle,
then eight. Boned and laced,
restricted, they do what they can.

A lending library. First women's
organization in the state. One place
they can vote. By 1879, the building.

Music, lectures and programs:
Horace Greeley, a phonograph
concert. Women who wanted

arts, and books and health
for Kalamazoo. Their motto,
Do what you can.

So they did. A day nursery,
school health programs. Literacy.
Today their sisters tend

the legacy: husband the building---
stained glass, gargoyle, the books.
They learn, they give,

they celebrate, they honor
the women who stretched and reached
and still do what they can.

-- Lynn Pattison, LLA member

Above: LLA scrapbook photo collage of special interest groups and projects.

In an age when women's clubs—and clubs in general—are disappearing from the scene, it is remarkable that the LLA continues to retain and add new members. The general membership is approximately 180 with a surprising number being active members. Even more surprising is the number of young women joining. Various reasons are given for this influx of youth. Some come for business networking, some for the chance to meet new people, some are intrigued by the sense of history of the building and the organization. Others join to share interests in the various activities available to members.

Social and educational activities open to members include book clubs, arts and culture, bridge, photography, needle crafters, and music appreciation. Current community outreach committees include the Books for Babies project and the Kalamazoo River Valley Trail committee. Books for Babies, is a philanthropic group that collects new and gently used books to give to various local agencies that serve young children. The goal is to expand the opportunities for literacy with children who may not have access to books and to encourage parents to read to their young ones. The group collects books throughout the year and twice yearly gathers to fill bags with hundreds of donated books. These are delivered to numerous agencies in Kalamazoo County. The Kalamazoo River Valley Trail committee meets to gather litter along a section of the trail near River Oaks Park.

In addition, once a year members gather at the LLA for a fun event known as "Muffins, Mittens, Soup and Sweets." Old wool sweaters are boiled down, cut up and sewn into mittens. Carla Noe-Emig provides the soup and sweets. In the past, these handmade mittens were passed onto Ministry with Community, the Kalamazoo Peace House, and the Kalamazoo Gospel Mission for distribution to their clients.

While all of the LLA groups and committees serve their own important niche, the Ways & Means Committee makes it possible for the LLA to continue to keep the doors open. Monthly, reasonably priced luncheons give members an opportunity to enjoy interesting programs and delicious food that has become the hallmark of the LLA. An ice cream social is held annually on the first Saturday in June. Doors are opened to the public and pies and other desserts are served along with ice cream. Tours of the landmark building are also given during that day and upon appointment. A holiday bazaar is held in November and all food is prepared and served by members of the Ways & Means Committee. In addition, the building is a popular venue available to rent for weddings, showers, anniversary parties, business meetings, music events, poetry readings, and other events. Proceeds from these gatherings pay for maintenance of the historic building.

The success of LLA events is not just about what happens in the kitchen. There are seven Ways & Means sub-committees, including Audiovisual, Docents, Linen Maintenance, Reservations, Decorations, Table Setting, and a Tea committee. These groups coordinate the food and desserts for the monthly LLA member luncheons and teas. This close-knit group of committees enjoys working together to put the best foot forward for guests.

Standing Committees also serve an important role in the LLA organization. Members of the Audit, Budget-Finance, Buildings &

Page 168: LLA scrapbook photos of special interest groups and projects.

Grounds, Bylaws, Community Outreach Evaluation (CORE), Filing, Marketing, Media, Membership, Nominating, and Program committees keep the business of the LLA on track.

The Buildings & Grounds is responsible for maintenance of the interior and exterior of the building. This includes keeping service contracts current, overseeing custodial duties, upkeep of the garden, and generally making sure that this historic building is in good working order. Subcommittees of Buildings & Grounds include the Historian, the Circulating Library, and the Vintage Library (in charge of the historical book collection). All of these committees work together to give the LLA vibrancy and relevance.

From the beginning of the LLA, the plan was not only to promote literacy in the village of Kalamazoo, but also to enlighten members and the community. Programs sponsored by LLA have included lectures on a wide range of topics. Lecturers came from the University of Michigan, Kalamazoo College, Western State Normal School, and area experts. Even the editor of the *New York Tribune* and political activist, Horace Greeley, was a guest lecturer.

These speaking events were an important source of revenue for the organization. Greeley's lecture alone brought in more than $400 to the LLA's coffers (Potts and Lyons-Jenness 1997, 14). However this was the exception. For the most part, throughout its history, the members struggled with finances. Yet even when they were low on income, the ladies felt the need to give charitable contributions. Over the years the LLA has given to a variety of causes. According to the *Centennial Booklet of 1952* written by Mrs. George E. Foote, the LLA purchased war bonds, adopted a French child, and contributed to the Save the Children's Federation. They gave annually to the community Christmas tree, the Lake Farm for Boys, the Cancer Society, and the Red Cross. They cooperated in the work of the USO during World War II, supported the Gray Ladies, contributed to the Memorial Highway project, the Percy Jones Veterans Hospital in Battle Creek, gave financial assistance to help furnish a recreation room for the Women's Army Auxiliary Corps of Des Moines, Iowa, and contributed to the Penny Art fund to help complete the art building at Interlochen, Michigan.

In 1967, a student loan fund was established by the LLA for use by Western Michigan University. Contributions to causes significantly increased after the Virginia Earl Endowment Fund was established in 2002. A scholarship fund began with significant financial help being given to worthy students. A report of 2010 lists 47 charitable organizations receiving financial contributions that year alone.

With the onset of the 21st Century Project fund drive, outside contributions ceased as the Board of Directors felt that asking for money from the community and foundations and then giving away money perhaps would seem to be a poor business practice. Now that the construction costs have been paid, the LLA hopes to return to the practice of making contributions that has been so much a part of its history.

So what is the heart and soul of the LLA? It is the laughter of the women in the kitchen working

※ Kitchen volunteer name tags.

together preparing a meal. It is the lively discussion of a book shared at a book club meeting. It is the healthy competition at a bridge tournament. It is the sense of satisfaction when an LLA event has been successful. It is the making of a new friend. It is the opportunity for women's individual talents to gain an outlet. It is women coming together who fully appreciate the history of the LLA and its beautiful building, who share an interest in the LLA's offerings to make the Kalamazoo community a better place to live. One hundred sixty-three years after its founding, the LLA continues to enrich the community and meet the educational and social needs of its members.

TIMELINE

1830	Titus Bronson plats the village of Bronson.
1836	The village is re-named Kalamazoo.
1837	Michigan becomes the 26th state of the union.
1843	Dr. James A. B. Stone and his wife, Lucinda Hinsdale Stone, arrive in Kalamazoo. Dr. Stone accepts the invitation to take charge of a new branch of the University of Michigan. The school eventually becomes Kalamazoo College.
1844	Mrs. Alexis Ransom and Mrs. Lyman Kendall decide to spend one afternoon a week reading to one another.
1844 ~ 1852	More than 2,000 books are collected.

1852 — An organizational meeting is held, and those eight present adopt a constitution for the Ladies' Library Association of Kalamazoo (LLA). A board of directors is nominated. Hannah Trask is the first librarian. The phrase "Do What You Can," is adopted as the LLA motto. The library is opened to the public. The LLA becomes the first women's club in Michigan and (as far as can be determined) is the third-oldest women's club in the country.

1855 — Mrs. D. B. (Ruth) Webster offers to donate a parcel of land as a permanent home for the library. Her offer is declined.

1859 — The LLA is incorporated.

1861 — The Civil War begins, and most of the ladies are involved with efforts to help Civil War soldiers.

1867 — Ruth Webster again, offers to donate a lot for the library. Again, her offer is declined.

1869 — Women are admitted to the University of Michigan.

173

1872 — The Kalamazoo Board of Education opens a public library in Firemen's Hall.

1873 — The Literary Club is organized under the direction of the LLA and Mrs. Lucinda Stone. The four sections (committees) of the club are Art and Literature, Science and Education, History, and Miscellaneous Committees.

1877 — When the treasury report reveals there is $3,814 in the Building Fund, the Board of Directors finally accepts Ruth Webster's offer of a lot on Park Street. Chicago architect Henry L. Gay, is immediately hired to design the building.

1878 — In November, the main structure is complete. Ruth Webster, charter member, treasurer and guiding force of the construction of the building, passes away.

1879 — The Ladies' Library Association of Kalamazoo, under a legislative act, is allowed the right to hold property to the amount of $30,000 (exclusive of books) without taxation. The building is dedicated on May 20, 1879.

1883 — The loan is paid and the building is independently owned by the Ladies' Library Association.

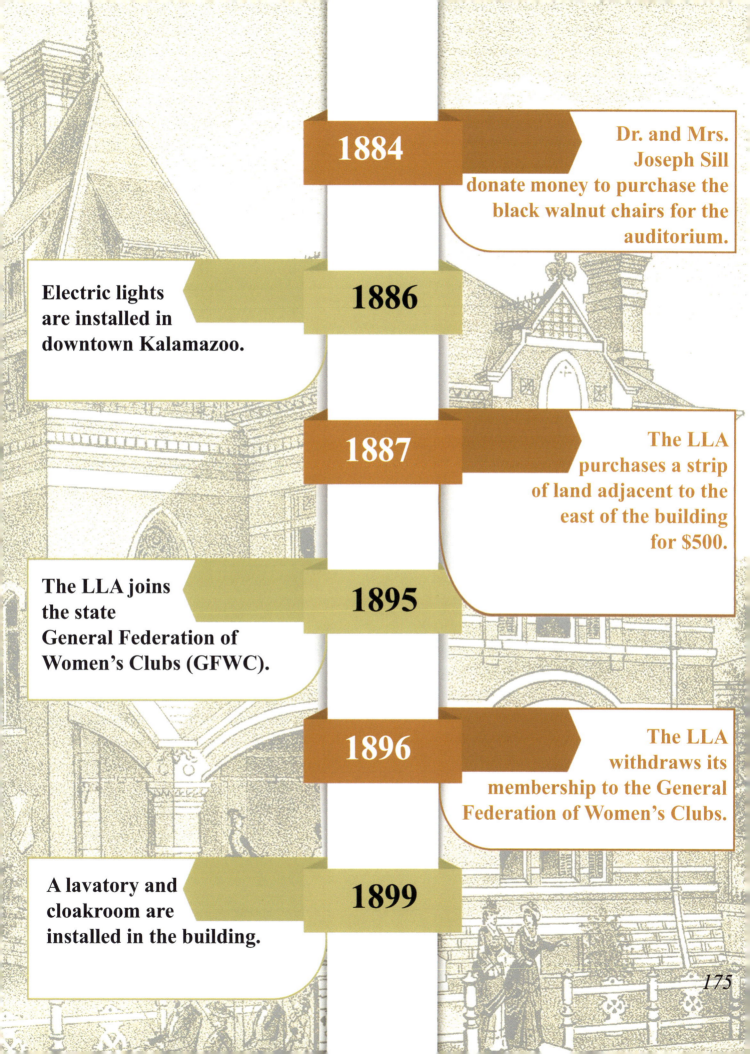

1884	Dr. and Mrs. Joseph Sill donate money to purchase the black walnut chairs for the auditorium.
1886	Electric lights are installed in downtown Kalamazoo.
1887	The LLA purchases a strip of land adjacent to the east of the building for $500.
1895	The LLA joins the state General Federation of Women's Clubs (GFWC).
1896	The LLA withdraws its membership to the General Federation of Women's Clubs.
1899	A lavatory and cloakroom are installed in the building.

1900 — Charter member Lucinda Hinsdale Stone dies. The Literary Club and the LLA join as one unit, which reflected the wishes of Mrs. Stone.

1902 — The LLA re-joins the state GFWC.

1903 — The LLA and the General Federation of Women's Clubs unite to establish the Lucinda Hinsdale Stone Scholarship Fund. A 12th century lead gargoyle from England is donated to the LLA by the dean of students at Kalamazoo Central High School, and placed outside the building as a downspout.

1905 — At the annual meeting, the club colors of gold and white are adopted. The Steinway piano is purchased for $825.

1917 — The United States enters World War I. LLA members knit countless socks and sweaters for soldiers. They raise money to purchase food items for army camps.

1920 — The 19th Amendment, allowing women the right to vote, is ratified.

1931 — The building of the kitchen addition begins, along with two bathrooms and two dressing rooms.

1941 — The United States enters World War II. As before, the ladies involve themselves as they help on the home front.

1946 ~ 1975 — This is a time marked by a great deal of fundraising, building maintenance, and the purchase of items for events.

1961 — The Michigan Historical Commission designates the building as an historic site. The gargoyle is stolen from the front of the building.

1962 — The gargoyle is returned, and is slightly damaged. It is repaired and placed in the main library room.

1970 — The LLA building is placed on the National Register of Historic Places.

1975 ~ 1979 — The first major building restoration project begins, and is completed.

1978 — A reproduction gargoyle made by Lee Wallace, is placed outside at the corner of the building.

1979 — In May, a celebration of the building's centennial is held.

1990 ~ 1991 — The second major restoration is completed.

2002 — The LLA receives a significant endowment from the estate of Virginia Earl. Although the Kalamazoo College teacher was never a member, she had attended meetings with her mother, who was a member.

2011
The LLA migrates into social media, with an expanded and comprehensive website (www.KalamazooLadiesLibrary.org) and a Facebook presence

(https://www.facebook.com/The-Ladies-Library-Association-of-Kalamazoo).

2012
The Board of Directors votes to begin construction to make the building barrier-free. Work begins to install a three-level elevator, four barrier-free bathrooms, and an entire upgrade of wiring (including building-wide Wi-Fi access), plus a fully-licensed kitchen. A loan of $1.5 million is obtained. A ground-breaking ceremony is held.

2013
The LLA is given designated funds to purchase a parking lot by James and Lois Richmond. The lot at 341 West Lovell Street, is south of the LLA building. The membership votes to de-federate from the GFWC.

2014
In May, the new addition is dedicated. The loan is paid off. The 341 West Lovell Street building is removed to make way for a dedicated LLA parking lot. A collection of vintage dresses is donated by Jerre James.

2015
The parking lot is paved and landscaped. New auditorium chairs are purchased and delivered.

GENERAL FEDERATION OF WOMEN'S CLUBS
GFWC HISTORY AND DE-FEDERATION

The mission statement of the General Federation of Women's Clubs is "an international organization dedicated to community improvement by enhancing the lives of others through volunteer service." Their club manual reports that GFWC's roots are traced back to 1868, when professional journalist Jane Cunningham Croly of New York City attempted to attend a lecture by novelist Charles Dickens at an all-male press club. She was denied entry on account of her gender. "Jennie June" formed a women's club, naming it Sorosis, a Greek word meaning "an aggregation; a sweet flavor of many fruits." Later, Sorosis members proposed a conference of women's clubs to pursue the cause of federation. Their combined efforts enabled the GFWC to grow and adapt to the changing lifestyles and concerns of women throughout the globe. These women's clubs formed the federation and combined their efforts.

The official motto of the GFWC was adopted in 1957 and reads "Unity in Diversity." This organization has been headquartered in Washington, D.C. since 1901. The Kalamazoo Ladies' Library Association established their organization with a similar framework of activities and community service. This included, but was not limited to, areas of arts, conservation, education, home life, international outreach, and public issues, as well as special projects in domestic violence awareness and prevention and advocacy for children.

Many members of the LLA participated in leadership roles with the GFWC, attending meetings, lectures, classes, receptions, and conventions throughout Michigan and other locations in the U.S. The LLA worked in collaboration with the GFWC in numerous fundraising activities supporting local and international organizations and projects. Many LLA members over the years benefited from club specific training in leadership, membership retention, parliamentary procedures, and other educational opportunities from the GFWC.

As the LLA became more independent and more community oriented, volunteer time and money became a concern. Many of the activities of the GFWC required volunteer resources and annual dues. Some members felt these resources were being used too much with the GFWC and were needed locally. The LLA directed more resources toward local community needs and established this as a priority. Some members felt it was not cost effective to pay dues to a national organization and felt the funds were more productive for operating costs and local charitable work.

Considerable discussion took place and the membership voted to de-federate from the GFWC in 2013 in order to concentrate their efforts in the local community. This was not the first time this had happened to the LLA. The organization first de-federated in 1896. The reason as best can be interpreted from board minutes was again because of funds and volunteer time required. The LLA rejoined GFWC in May 1902.

After the 2013 de-federation, a group of LLA members formed a new GFWC group in Kalamazoo. It is called the Kalamazoo Area Women's Club-GFWC. They are active in assisting the national organization with local, state, and international projects and issues. They remain dedicated to the tradition of community improvement by enhancing the lives of others through volunteer service in the areas of arts, conservation, education, home life, international outreach, and public issues. Many of their members retained their membership in the LLA as well as the new GFWC group. That group's membership has increased and charitable work with the GFWC continues through them.

The decision to de-federate caused some discord within the LLA, but history has shown the LLA to be a strong organization and has managed to deal with numerous difficulties over the test of time. If history repeats itself, efforts to rejoin the federation could occur in the future. The LLA continues to support more local charitable work and community outreach.

The club Collect originated with the affiliation of the LLA with the GFWC. Today the Collect is still recited as a group at the first business meeting of each month of the Ladies' Library Association.

The Collect

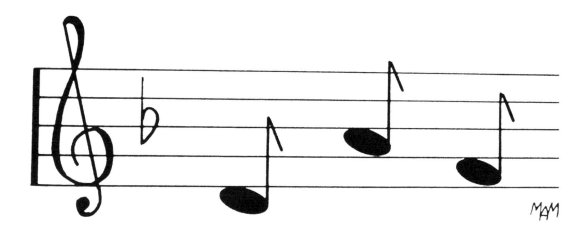

Musical Setting
by
NORA B. SCHOONMAKER

●

Published by
LADIES LIBRARY ASSN.
333 South Park Street
Kalamazoo, Mich.

A COLLECT FOR CLUBWOMEN

Keep us, oh God, from pettiness;
Let us be large in thought, in word, in deed.

Let us be done with faultfinding
and leave off self-seeking.

May we put away all pretense
and meet each other face to face,
without self-pity and without prejudice.
May we never be hasty in judgement
and always be generous.

Let us take time for all things;
make us to grow calm, serene, gentle.

Teach us to put into action our better impulses,
straight forward and unafraid.

Grant that we may realize it is
the little things that create differences,
that in the big things of life we are at one.

And may we strive to touch and to know
the great, common human heart of us all.

And, oh Lord God, let us forget not to be kind!

-- Mary Stewart, April 1904

About The Authors

Top left to right: Lisa Salay, Vanita Aloisio, Sharon Carlson, Judy Sherrod
Middle left to right: Deborah M. Killarney, Barbara Baker
Bottom left to right: Carla J. Noe-Emig, and Lois I. Richmond

Vanita Aloisio joined the LLA in 2010 and immediately began working in the kitchen as a member of the Ways & Means Committee and serving as a docent. She has researched extensively about the stained-glass windows and the art collection, and she is a member of the Lens Ladies' Artistry. Vanita earned a Bachelor's degree in education from Western Michigan University, a Master's degree in classroom teaching from Michigan State University, and library certification from the University of Michigan. She was a teacher-librarian for 27 years for Gull Lake Community Schools and for three years at Mattawan Schools, retiring in 2001. Recreationally, she enjoys family activities with her 12 grandchildren and photographing public art. She loves to play tennis, watch movies, and travel with her husband Mike.

Barbara Baker has been a community volunteer in Michigan since 2000, serving on several boards as secretary. Some of these organizations include: Quota International, Voluntary Action Center, VNA Quality Assurance Committee, Hospital Hospitality House, Kalamazoo County Parks Foundation, and Kalamazoo Advocates for Senior Issues. She joined LLA in 2003. Since 2006 she served as LLA's chairperson of the Ways & Means Committee and Event Planner. She also volunteered on the 21st Century Construction, Budget and Finance, and Building & Grounds Committees. She graduated from the University of Kansas with a BA degree in occupational therapy. She worked in this field in Kansas, Illinois, and Indiana before moving to Michigan. There she worked as Director of Rehabilitation Departments at Borgess Medical Center and as Disability Network-Client Services Manager until her retirement in 2000. She is married and has two daughters. Hobbies include sewing / handwork, photographing nature, cooking, and traveling with her husband.

Sharon Carlson joined the Ladies' Library Association in 2005. She earned a Ph.D. in United States history from Western Michigan University in 2002. Her dissertation title is Ladies' Library Associations of Michigan: Women, Reform, and Use of Public Space. She also has graduate degrees in library science from Wayne State University and public administration from Western Michigan University. She is employed at Western Michigan University as an associate professor in the university libraries where she directs the archives and regional history collections. She also teaches an upper level public history course, Archival Administration. She serves as historian for the Kalamazoo Ladies' Library Association and volunteers as a hostess for events. She was a research consultant for this publication.

Deborah M. Killarney joined the LLA in 2011 and jumped in with both feet. Her roles included creating an electronic member database; revamping and expanding the LLA website; producing and editing the bi-monthly newsletter; producing the annual member yearbook; and serving on the audiovisual committee. She also served on the Board of Directors as secretary and established the Lens Ladies' Artistry (a photography club within the LLA). Deb retired from the education department of United Airlines, volunteered in community theatre for over 20 years, earned an advanced associates degree in web design from Kalamazoo Valley Community College, wrote and photographed for a regional magazine in the San Francisco area, and established a community garden in Kalamazoo. She is still active in LLA and several community service projects.

Carla J. Noe-Emig became a member of the Ladies' Library Association in 2011. She holds an undergraduate and two graduate degrees from Western Michigan University (1977 Bachelor of Science, Psychology and Secondary Education; 1988 Master of Arts, Organizational Communications; 1997 Master of Arts, Human Resource Development). Professionally she has worked as an administrator of Experience Based Education for Kalamazoo Valley Community College and author of the EBE Express monthly newsletter; job development specialist, grant writer, and CETA program director for the W.E. Upjohn Institute; vocational specialist for International Rehabilitation Associates; instructor for Western Michigan University (Distributive Education and Fashion Merchandising programs); owner and manager of C.J. Radrags; and currently as co-owner and manager of W.M. Spaman Jewellers, South Street Properties, and PhotoJoy Studio. Her LLA involvement has included writing newsletter articles; chairing Home Life, Nominations, Mitten Ministry, and Scrapbook committees; co-chairing Holiday Bazaar and New Year's Fest committees; serving as LLA wedding coordinator; member directory photographer; and member of the audio-visual, program, conservation, and Park Trades Art Hop committees. Other affiliations include General Federations of Women's Clubs, Kalamazoo Area Women's Club, and the Midwest Miniatures Museum. Leisure activities include: vegetarian cooking, book and music appreciation groups, crafting, volunteer service, vintage campers, historic building restoration, family time, and photography. Her photographs have appeared in local print media and national magazine publications. She has also received state and national photographic awards.

Lois I. Richmond joined the LLA in 2002. She graduated from the Bronson School of Nursing and worked as a Registered Nurse at Bronson Hospital for 33 years, retiring in 1987 as Assistant Vice President of Nursing Administration. During her career at Bronson Hospital, she coordinated numerous construction projects as the nurse consultant. She graduated from Western Michigan University with a Bachelor of Science degree in health studies. In 2011, she received the Distinguished Alumni Award from the College of Health and Human Services and was inducted into the Alumni Academy. Offices held in the LLA: Chair of the Arts Appreciation Committee, First Vice President, President (2012-2013), and Past President (2014-2015). She served on the Budget / Finance Committee, supervised the 21st Century Project, and chaired the Building & Grounds Committee. Other affiliations include Kalamazoo Audubon Society, Wild Ones (charter member), Kalamazoo Nature Center, and Southwest Michigan Land Conservancy. As a self-taught naturalist, Lois taught nature classes and led field trips for many years. She is the author of The Missing Gargoyle of the Ladies' Library, a book of historic fiction published in 2014. Lois and her husband have focused their philanthropy on education, the arts, community needs, and the LLA. Hobbies include watercolor painting and various crafts.

Lisa Salay has been a member of the LLA since 2008. She was a board member for two years as Public Issues Chair and served on numerous committees for the LLA. Lisa currently serves on a number of nonprofit boards and committees in the Kalamazoo area. She utilized her biology degree in the healthcare field for over 20 years. Lisa enjoys traveling, reading, music, and gardening.

Judy Sherrod is the retired Executive Director of the Volunteer Center of Kalamazoo. She is a graduate of Western Michigan University with a BA in English and a Master's Degree in Guidance and Counseling. She taught English at the middle school and college level. In addition she was the Director of Annual Campaigns and Events for the Kalamazoo County Chapter of the American Red Cross. Judy served as a board member on numerous community nonprofit organizations. Her lifelong love of history prompted her to join the LLA in 2008. Besides being an LLA board member, she served on the 21st Century Construction Committee, Capital Campaign Committee, 341 Committee, Buildings & Grounds Committee, and served as Docent for several years. In her spare time, she is an avid reader, enjoys helping friends with interior design, and loves spending time with family including her young grandson.

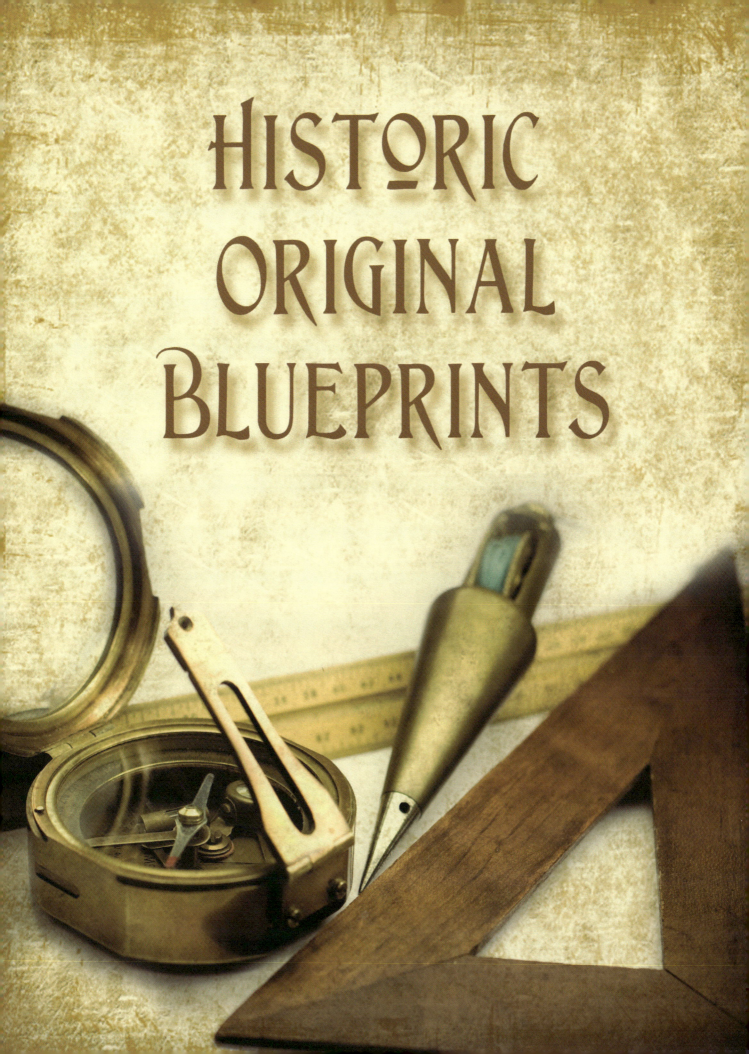

✱ Blueprints dated July 31, 1878.

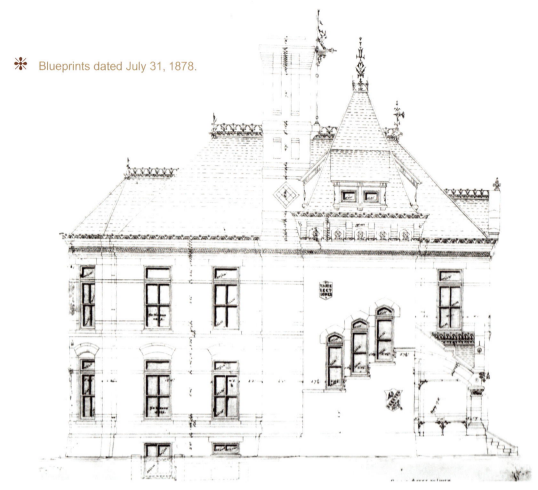

Right Flank Elevation

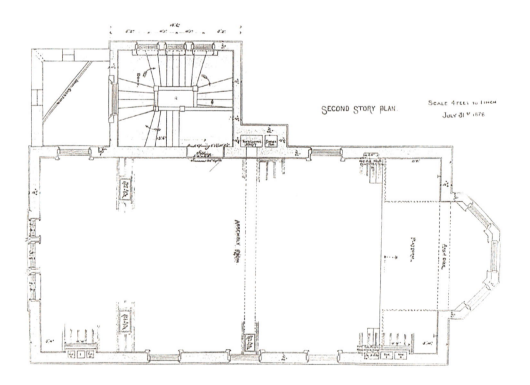

190

BIBLIOGRAPHY

Accessible Archives, Inc. April 7, 2011. www.accessible-archives.com (accessed September 2015).

Agnew, John Holmes and Bidwell, Walter H. "Women Physicians." *Eclectic Magazine of Foreign Literature, Science and Art* 8 (1868): 1313.

Amanti Art. http://www.amantiart.com/search/?doSearch.x=0&doSearch.y=0&doSearch=Search&searchTerms=LadyLaFornarina&sortType=Popularity&currentPage=1&crumbs=&itemsPerPage=12&alt= (accessed April 22, 2015).

Andover's Architectural Styles. preservation.mhl.org (accessed September 22, 2015).

"Antinous." *The New Encyclopaedia Britannica.* Vol. 1. Chicago: Encyclopaedia Britannica, 2010, 458.

Bleier, Paul & Meta Bleier. *John Rogers' Groups of Statuary: A Pictorial & Annotated Guide for the Collector.* New York: Paul and Meta Bleier, 1976.

Bolton, Henry Carrington. "Early Practice of Medicine by Women." *Journal of Science*, January 1881, 8.

Carlson, Sharon Ph.D. *Ladies' Library Association of Michigan: Women, Reform, and Use of Public Spaces.* Kalamazoo, MI: Western Michigan University, 2002.

"Dante Alighieri." *The New Encyclopaedia Britannica.* Vol. 16. Chicago: Encyclopaedia Britannica, 2010, 972.

den Bleyker, Mrs. John. *Compendium of History and Biography of Kalamazoo County, Michigan.* Editors David Fisher and Frank Little. Chicago: A. W. Bowen & Company, 1906.

Dunbar, Willis. *Kalamazoo and How it Grew.* Kalamazoo, MI: Western Michigan College, 1952.

Durant, Samuel. *The History of Kalamazoo County.* Kalamazoo: Everts & Abbott, 1880.

Dykema, Dorothy. "LLA Garden Dedication Address." 2002.

—. "Maintenance Verification Form for the State Historic Preservation Office." March 1, 2006.

—. Interview by 2015 Committee. *Past President and House Chair* (May 2015).

Dykema, Herman, comp. "28 Stained Glass Windows of Ladies' Library Association." May 15, 1996.

"Henrietta Maria." *The New Encyclopaedia Britannica.* Vol. 5. Chicago: Encyclopaedia Britannica, 2010, 833.

Houghton, Lynn Smith, and Pamela Hall O'Connor. *Kalamazoo Lost and Found.* Edited by Maria A. Perez-Stable. Kalamazoo, MI: This Kalamazoo Historic Preservation Commission, Kalamazoo, Michigan, 2001.

House of Antique Hardware. http://www.houseofantiquehardware.com/twist-doorbell (accessed August 2015).

Inflation Calculator. http://www.davemanuel.com/inflation-calculator.php (accessed June 2015).

Kalamazoo Chapter of The Embroiderers Guild of America. "1830 Kalamazoo 1980." *A Sesquicentennial Tapestry.* Kalamazoo, MI, 1980.

Kalamazoo College Alumnus. *Kalamazoo College Alumnus.* Vol. Winter Issue. Kalamazoo: Kalamazoo College, 1957.

Kalamazoo Daily Telegraph. November 16, 1895.
    —. "Ladies' Library Association." January 19, 1881, 4.

Kalamazoo Gazette. February 6, 1949.
—. November 23, 1971.
—. "Dedication of Ladies' Library Re-enacted." May 1979.
—. "Ladies' Library Association." January 9, 1883, 4.

—. "Obituaries." October 27, 1999, C4: 4.

—. "Sudden Death." November 30, 1878, 4.

—. "This City First Place to Make Portland Cement in Whole United States." November 19, 1911.

Kalamazoo Public Library, Name Files, "Otis A. Earl."

Kalamazoo Valley Museum Magazine. "Ladies' Soldiers Aid Society." Summer 2014, 8.

Leiby, James M. "Last One Standing: Michigan's Dower Law." Michigan State University College of Law, 2010, 2-3.

Ladies' Library Association Documents

LLA "Seventy-Five Years: L.L.A." Summary. 1927.

LLA 1858 Annual Report. January 1859.

LLA 1880 Annual Meeting Minutes. January 8, 1881.

LLA 1882 Annual Meeting Minutes. *Kalamazoo Gazette.* 1983.

LLA 1882 Annual Report. January 5, 1883.

LLA 1891 Constitution. 1891.

LLA 1997 House Committee Report.

LLA 1999 House & Grounds Annual Report. 2000.

LLA 2001-2002 President's Report. 2002.

LLA 2002-2003 House Committee Annual Report. 2003.

LLA 2006-2007 House Committee Annual Report. 2007.

LLA 2007-2008 House Committee Annual Report. 2008.

LLA Board of Directors October 26, 1878 Meeting Minutes. January 1859.

—. July 14, 1931, 43.

—. January 6, 1872.

—. August 17, 1878.

—. February 2, 1872.

—. January 6, 1872.

—. 2002-2013.

—. 1859.

—. 1882-1883.

LLA Celebration Week Program. 2012.

LLA Centennial Program. 1952.

LLA Dedication Program. 2014.

LLA Docent Handbook. Compiled by Judy Sherrod. May 2014.

LLA Historical Restoration Program. 1974-1980.

LLA Membership Lists. 1914-1941.

LLA Newsletter. November-December 2014, 6.

Michigan Pioneer and Historical Society. *An Account of Kalamazoo County.* Edited by Charles A Weissert. http://quod.lib.umich.edu/m/micounty/ARH7743.0001.001?rgn=main;view=fulltext;q1=Kalamazoo+County++Mich. (accessed August 7, 2015).

National Women's History Museum. *Footnotes.* https://www.nwhm.org/online-exhibits/votesforwomen/footnotes.html (accessed August 10, 2015).

Nave, Nelson, interview by Lisa Salay. *Architect* (September 2015).

Opdyke, Valerie. April 3, 2013.

Perry, Belle McArthur. *Lucinda Hinsdale Stone: Her Life Story and Reminiscences.* Detroit: The Blinn Publishing Co., 1902.

Pioneer Society of the State of Michigan. *Pioneer Collections.* Vol. III. Lansing, 1881.

Potts, Grace J, and Cheryl Lyons-Jenness. *Women with a Vision.* Kalamazoo: Ladies' Library Association, 1997.

Rife, Jamie. September 14, 2015.

Robertson, John. *Adjutant General's Department.* W. S. George & Co., 1882.

Sand Atlas. http://www.sandatlas.org/limestone/ (accessed August 2015).

Schmitt, Peter J. *Kalamazoo: 19th Century Homes in a Midwestern Village.* Kalamazoo, MI: Kalamazoo Historical Commission, 1976.

Sheridan, Helen. "The Art Collection: Stained Glass, Paintings, Sculpture." Ladies' Library Association, 2002.

Stanley, Caroline. "A Successful Woman's Club." *The New England Magazine*, March 1890, 54-62.

Stone, Lucinda Hinsdale, comp.
—. "Fine Arts in Kalamazoo." *Kalamazoo Daily Telegraph*, August 30, 1872, 4.
—. "Saturday Talks." *Kalamazoo Daily Telegraph*, October 14, 1882.
Stone, Lucinda Hinsdale. "The Ladies' Gallery." *Kalamazoo Daily Telegraph*, September 24, 1872, 4.

Theoi Greek Mythology. June 2011. http://www.theoi.com (accessed March 21, 2015).

Vittoria Colonna. www.female-genius.com (accessed February 18, 2015).

"Vittoria Colonna." *The New Encyclopaedia Britannica.* Vol. 3. Chicago: Encyclopedia Britannica, 2010, 465.

All historical Ladies' Library Association documents referred to in this book are filed at the Charles C. and Lynn L. Zhang Legacy Collections Center at Western Michigan University in Kalamazoo, Michigan. More recent documents are filed at the Ladies' Library Association Building.

INDEX

A

Abraham Lincoln and the Council of War, 84, 85

Acknowledgements, viii

Acoustics, 52, 113, 142

Act of the Legislature (1879), 8, 11

ADA, 130, 133, 139, 144

Addition, 5, 7, 11, 44, 47, 50, 51, 70-73, 91, 95, 97, 105, 110, 112, 138-141, 148, 168, 177, 179, 188

Alley Agreement, 11, 141

Aloisio, Vanita, vii, 185, 186

Americans with Disabilities Act, 130

Anniversary, 45, 82, 88, 90, 106, 113, 114, 158, 159, 161, 168

Anthony, Susan B., xviii, 39

Antinous, 82, 83, 192

Aphrodite, 82

Apollo Belvedere, 82, 83

Architect, vi, viii, xiii, 5, 15, 16, 19, 23, 45, 57, 109, 132, 139, 142, 144, 153, 158, 174, 192, 195

Architecture, vi, viii, 5, 109

Art Deco, 51

Aspdin, Joseph, 16

Auditorium, vi, 27, 48, 50, 52, 53, 58, 67, 73, 94, 95, 96, 113, 121, 123, 125, 142, 163, 175, 179

Austin & Tomlinson, 30

B

Baird, Anna, 112

Baker, Barbara, vii, 85, 132, 140, 163, 185, 186

Baker, Richard, viii, 132, 139

Barrier-Free, vi, 128, 145, 179

Basement, 30, 42, 45, 47, 57, 121, 142, 143, 146, 148

Bauman, Barry, 85
Billingham, Blanche, 19
Board Minutes, 32, 42, 139, 180
Books for Babies, 113, 167
Borsos, Robert B., 159
Boundaries, 141
Bower, Mary, 132
Brees, Mrs. Henry, 113
Bronson Hospital, 132, 187
Bronson, Titus, xiv, 172
Brooker, Katharine, 160
Brown, Helen Lukan, 161
Brown, Mary C., 159
Browning, Elizabeth Barrett, 33, 93
Bryan, William Jennings, 85
Bryant, William Cullen, 92
Buckhout, Jim, 57, 140
Buildings & Grounds, 168, 169, 188
Burns, Robert, 95
Bush and Paterson, 7
Bush, Frederick, vi

C
Cadman, Mrs. John, 100
Callahan, Tim, 111
Carlson, Sharon, vii, 140, 144, 185, 186
Celebration, xiv, 45, 62, 156, 158, 159, 160, 161, 163, 178, 195
Chadborn, Irene, 44
Chairs, 47, 53, 121, 130, 175, 179
Chandelier, xiii, 35, 52, 54, 55, 139
Church, xiv, xvi, 7, 30, 37, 85, 90, 95, 125, 130, 141, 145, 153
Circulating Library, vi, 44, 169

Civil War, vi, xiii, xviii, xix, 72, 84, 106, 173
Clark, Anna, 37
Clothing, Vintage, 44
Colonna, Vittoria, 105
Conner, Reverend Wayne, 85
Conte, Louis and Annette, 27
Contractor, 7, 73, 141, 144
Cooky Book, 73
Copper, James Fenimore, xiv, 33, 94
Cottrell, June, 160
Croly, Jane Cunningham, 180
Cupid, 82, 110

D
Dante, 95, 97, 100, 101, 192, 198
Dante and Beatrice, 100, 101
Dare to Know, 160
Dedication, x, 11, 50, 153, 159, 161, 193, 195
DeGroot, Ethel and Thomas, 52
den Bleyker, Mrs. John, 192
Dennison, Mrs. William, 121
Dickens, Charles, 94, 180
Dressing Rooms, 50, 51, 73, 138, 177
Dykema, Dorothy, 193
Dykema, Herman (Herm), 32, 96, 130

E
Earl, Virginia, 111, 136, 153, 159, 169, 178
Eastlake, 23, 53
Elevator, 113, 132, 133, 139, 144, 148, 179
Embroiderers Guild, Kalamazoo Chapter, 113, 193
Emig, Nick, viii

Endsley, Bernadine, 27
Entry, 7, 20, 22, 23, 25, 32, 37, 57, 58, 130, 132, 180
Erie Canal, xiv
Eschelbach, Tim, 153

F

Ferraro, Lance, 111, 136
Ferraro, Sharon, viii
Fireman's Hall, 30, 100
First Baptist Church, 30
First Presbyterian Church, 85, 141, 153
Fisher, Eliza, xix
Foote, Mrs. George E., 169
Foyer, 20, 22, 23, 25, 27, 32, 73, 100, 124, 132, 133, 142
Fredricks, Edgar, 159
Freeland, Annmarie and Wesley, 153
Fundraiser, 19, 138

G

Garden, 112, 130, 132, 136, 141, 150, 153, 155, 158, 159, 160, 163, 169, 187, 188, 193
Gargoyle, 19, 37, 45, 166, 176, 177, 178, 187
Gay, Henry L., 5, 174
General Federation of Women's Clubs, 111, 159, 175, 180
Gibbs, Mrs. K. May, 121
Gilmore Foundation, 140
Gilmore, Mrs. Donald, 109
Godey's Lady's Book, 112
Goldsmith, Oliver, 95
Gothic Revival, 15
Grant, Ulysses S., 84
Great American Women Figurine Doll Collection, 85

Greeley, Horace, 166, 169
Gregg, Richard, 109
Gruss, Karen, 140

H
Hadrian, 82
Hale, Sarah Josepha, 112
Harold and Grace Upjohn Foundation, 140
Harris, Elizabeth, 160
Hawthorne, Nathaniel, 94
Hinsdale, Aaron, xvi
Hollins, Sean and Sonya, viii
Holst, Laurits, 108, 109
Houghton, Lynn, viii
Hurd, Alice, 160

I
Irving, Washington, 93

J
James, Jerre, 179
Jamison, Frank, 50, 160
Jamison, Paula, 144, 160
Jensen, Gregory, 141
Jim's Arch, 56, 57

K
Kalafut, Grace Anne, 44
Kalamazoo Central High School, 37, 136, 176
Kalamazoo Civic, 11, 50, 73, 132, 141
Kalamazoo College, xvi, 100, 111, 136, 169, 172, 178, 193
Kalamazoo Foundation, 73

Kalamazoo Gazette, xiv, 4, 17, 37, 105, 109, 136, 159, 193, 194
Kalamazoo Institute of Arts, viii, 92, 144
Kalamazoo Network, 155
Kalamazoo Public Library, 30, 32, 90, 136, 194
Kalamazoo Public Museum, 37
Kars, Marge, viii
Kedzie, Mrs. A. S., 121
Kendall, Mrs. Lyman, xiv, 121
Killarney, Deborah, vii, 185, 186
Kinch, Beth, 125
Kitchen, 47, 50, 70, 72, 73, 93, 125, 132, 138, 139, 140, 142, 144, 148, 164, 168, 169, 170, 177, 179, 186
Kreidler, Mary Jane, 91

L

La Fornarina, 106
Ladies' Soldiers Aid Society, xix, 194
Lawton, Charles DeWitt, 126
Lawton, Lucy Lovina Latham, 126
LeBrun, Madame, 100, 103
La Fornarina, 106
Lending Library, 30, 32, 39, 40, 43, 44, 45, 85, 93, 110, 125, 138, 166
Lincoln, Abraham, 84, 85
Lincoln, Robert Todd, 84
Lines of Knowledge, 42, 90, 93, 96, 142, 159
Longfellow, Henry Wadsworth, 20, 92
Luna, Judge Marjorie, 52

M

Main Library, 28, 30, 32, 39, 77, 89, 92, 100, 106, 120, 121, 123, 125, 133, 136, 163, 177
Mangee, Mrs. Charles, 125

Mason, Mrs. G. H., 82, 98
Maurice, Alfred P., 109
McCann, Sean, 161
Michelangelo, 80, 95, 96, 105
Michigan Historical Commission, xiii
Michigan Stained Glass Census, 96
Michigan State Sanitary Fair, xix
Miller-Davis Construction, 139
Mills, Florence G., 79, 159
Milton, John, 96, 97
Miscellaneous Collections, 42
Mitchell, Lucinda, xvi
Moorish Style, 89
Mountain Home Cemetery, xviii, 5, 16
Mulders Moving & Storage, 140

N

National Register of Historic Places, vi, x, xiii, 177
Nave, Nelson, viii, 15, 132, 139, 140
Nave's Cave, 142
Nehil and Sivak, 139
Noe-Emig, Carla, vii, 168, 185, 187
Norton, Virginia, 123
Novella D'Andrea, 94

O

O. F. Miller Construction, 73
O'Brien, Margaret, 161
Oak Openings, xiv
Old Home Rehabilitation Company, 142
Opdyke, Valerie, 126, 127, 195
Owen Group, 140

P

Paintings, viii, 52, 85, 98, 100, 101, 105, 108, 110, 116, 139, 158, 196
Parsons, Honorable J., 5
Parzyck, Roger, 54
Pattison, Lynn, 166
Peck Shell Collection, 43
Porch, 16, 19, 37
Portage Garden Club, 155
Portland Cement, 16, 194
Pottawatomi Indians, 113
Potter, Mrs. John (Ruth), xix
President's Room, 50, 54, 73
Psyche, 82

Q

Queen Anne Style, 7
Queen Henrietta, 106

R

Ransom, Mrs. Alexis, xiv, 121, 172
Recipes, 19, 73, 112
Rice, Colonel George, 30
Rice, Susan, 30, 121
Richmond, James, 50, 53
Richmond, Lois, vii, 37, 54, 132, 140, 144, 145, 160, 161, 179, 185, 187
Rife, Corwin, 37
Rife, Jamie, 195
Roberts, Tamara, 125
Robinson, David, 111
Rodewald, Herbert and Fern, 90, 159
Rogers, John (Groups), 84, 85
Ross, Dr. Barry, 52
Roussi, Chris, viii

S

Safe Harbor, 108, 109
Salay, Lisa, vii, 55, 140, 185, 188, 195
Schaeffer, Nora, 52
Scheer, Robin Leva, 109
Scheffer, Ary, 101
Schlegel, Topsy, 140
Sculpture, viii, 80, 82, 84, 85, 140, 153, 196
Shakespeare, William, 95
Shane, Shirley, 90, 91, 125, 132, 140
Sheridan, Helen, viii, 92
Sherrod, Judy, vii, 140, 185, 188, 195
Sill, Joseph, 53, 175
Sheridan, Helen, viii, 92
Sorosis, 180
Stage, vi, 5, 7, 27, 52, 53, 54, 55, 58, 94, 95, 96, 123, 142
Stained Glass, viii, 86, 88, 91, 96, 97, 166, 193, 196
Stanley, Caroline, 92
Stanton, Elizabeth Cady, 39
Stanton, Elwin W., 84, 85
Start, Elizabeth, 161
Statuary, 37, 80, 85, 100, 153, 192
Stewart, Mary, 184
Stone, Caroline Moore, 105, 108
Stone, Clement Walker, 105
Stone, Lucinda Hinsdale, vi, xvi, xviii, 39, 82, 108, 121, 127, 176, 195
Stucki, Naomi, Marcia, and Heidi, 50
Subscription library, 30
Sybils, 105
Symbol, 37, 39, 89, 91, 94, 153

T

Tambroni, Clotolde, 93, 94

Tennyson, Lord Alfred, 95

The Missing Gargoyle of the Ladies' Library, 37, 187

The Women's Window, 93, 94

Thomas, Daniel, 4

Time capsule, 45

Transoms, 88, 92, 93, 94, 95, 97

U

University of Bologna, 94

University of Michigan, xvi, 126, 136, 169, 172, 173, 186

V

Van Blaricom, Janice, 52

Van Dyke, Anthony, 106

Van Haaften, Ruth, 123

Venetian Gothic Style, vi, 7

Venus, 42, 82, 83

Vigneau, Loretta Dingeman, 112

W

W. H. Wells & Bros. Glass Co., 88

W. S. and Lois Van Dalson Foundation, 140

Wagner, Laura V., 11

Walker, Mrs. J. W., 123

Wallace, Lee, 19, 37, 178

Ware, James and Sheila, 52

Ware, Margaret, 52

Ways & Means, 73, 140, 158, 163, 168, 186

Webster, Daniel, 85

Webster, Judge D. B., 4

Webster, Ruth, (Mrs. Judge D. B.), vi, xxii, 4, 5, 7, 34, 88, 89, 100, 119, 136, 173

Welborn, Robert, 159

Westnedge, Joseph P., 108

Westnedge, Mary, 108

Whittier, John Greenleaf, 92, 93

Williams, Dr. D. Terry, 52

Windows See: Stained Glass, viii, 86, 88, 91, 96, 97, 166, 193, 196

Wolbers, Betty, 73, 91, 155

Women with a Vision, 158, 195

Women's Declaration of Sentiments, 127

Women's Suffrage Movement, 39

Wortley, Mrs. Alfred, 85

Y

Yellow roses, 39, 91

Z

Zhang Legacy Collections, viii, 62, 140, 196

CPSIA information can be obtained at www.ICGtesting.com
Printed in the USA
BVIW12n1159230416
445208BV00001B/1